Norse Mythology for Beginners:

Unveil the Legendary World of Norse Gods, Heroes, and Mythical Beasts. Explore the Epic Tales of Creation, Destruction, and the Fabled Battle of Ragnarok.

ETHAN CRAFTWELL

BAMBOO CIRCLE
— BOOKS —

bamboo-circle.com

Welcome to 'Norse Mythology for Beginners.'

As a token of our appreciation for your interest in this captivating journey, we've created something special just for you.

Scan the QR code below to access our exclusive e-book, featuring 10 divine recipes inspired by the myths and gods of Norse mythology.

TABLE OF CONTENTS

INTRODUCTION:
EXPLORING THE WORLD OF NORSE MYTHOLOGY

Welcome to Norse Mythology

Welcome to the rugged, windswept world of Norse mythology—a land where gods walk among men, giants wage wars against the heavens, and epic heroes carve their names into the heart of legend. Norse mythology is not just a collection of ancient stories; it is the essence of a culture built on honor, courage, and the acceptance of fate. Much like the myths of Greece and Egypt, these tales have shaped an entire civilization, influencing the Vikings' way of life and leaving an indelible mark on history.

But what makes Norse mythology truly captivating? Perhaps it is the looming presence of **Odin**, the Allfather, who sacrificed his eye for wisdom and waits for the inevitable twilight of the gods. Or maybe it's **Thor**, the thunder god, whose mighty hammer **Mjolnir** defends both gods and men from monstrous forces. The trickster **Loki** stirs chaos wherever he goes, while the fierce **Freyja** rules over love and battle with equal passion. Together, they inhabit Asgard, a realm high above Midgard, the world of humans, and serve as the pillars of a universe teeming with magic, mystery, and destiny.

Yet, Norse mythology is not just about gods. It is also a tale of mythical creatures that roam these lands, creatures such as **Fenrir**, the monstrous wolf prophesied to bring about the end of the world, and **Jormungandr**, the world serpent that encircles Midgard. These beings are not mere figments of imagination; they embody the untamable forces of nature and fate that the Vikings both revered and feared.

As you journey through these pages, you'll explore not only the divine realms of **Asgard** and **Vanaheim** but also the darker, more mysterious places like **Jotunheim**, home of the giants, and **Hel**, the land of the dead. Each realm, filled with its own gods, creatures, and untold wonders, weaves together to create a cosmos rich in lore and intrigue.

In many ways, Norse mythology mirrors the cultural and spiritual foundations found in Greek and Egyptian myths. Just as the Greeks looked to **Zeus** and **Hades**, and the Egyptians revered **Ra** and **Osiris**, the Norse placed their faith in a pantheon of gods who governed life, death, and everything in between. But where the Egyptians saw life as a cycle and the Greeks glorified heroism, the Norse embraced fate in all its forms, even when it promised destruction at the hands of **Ragnarok**—the great battle that would end the world as they knew it. Fate, for the Norse, was not something to be avoided, but met with courage and strength.

What lies ahead in this book are epic tales of bravery, betrayal, and cosmic battles that stretch across the Nine Realms. You will stand alongside mighty gods and cunning heroes as they face trials that will push them to their limits. You will witness the rise of legends, the fall of empires, and the fated clash between order and chaos. Each chapter will draw you deeper into the heart of this mystical world, where the stakes are as high as the heavens and as vast as the oceans.

Are you ready to step into a world where thunder roars, swords clash, and destiny awaits at the end of every path? The stories you're about to read aren't just myths—they are invitations to a time when gods and men shared the same fate, and the line between reality and legend blurred under the northern lights. The adventure begins now.

How This Book Will Guide You Through the Myths and Legends

This book is designed to be your companion as you explore the enthralling world of Norse mythology. Whether you are just beginning your journey into these ancient tales or are looking to deepen your understanding, the chapters ahead will guide you through the core elements of Norse myth, step by step.

Each chapter is organized to make these stories clear and engaging, offering not only detailed retellings of the myths but also summaries and key takeaways that highlight the themes and lessons behind the legends. To enhance your experience, you'll find **high-quality black and white illustrations** throughout the book, bringing to life the gods, heroes, and mythical creatures that define Norse mythology.

These striking visuals, from intricate **maps of the Nine Realms** to depictions of cosmic battles and legendary beasts, add depth to the stories and help you better understand the cosmic structure of the Norse universe. At the end of each chapter, quizzes will test your knowledge and deepen your engagement with the material, turning learning into an interactive and visually enriching experience.

This book aims to do more than just recount tales; it seeks to uncover the deeper meaning behind the myths, showing how they reflected the values, beliefs, and fears of the ancient Norse people. By the time you finish, you will have gained not only a knowledge of these incredible stories but also an understanding of how they continue to resonate in modern times.

Connecting the Legends: From Greece and Egypt to Norse

If you've explored the world of **Greek** and **Egyptian mythology** in our previous books, you'll notice both familiar themes and striking differences as you delve into Norse mythology. Like the Greeks and Egyptians, the Norse people used their myths to explain the mysteries of life, the cosmos, and the divine. But where the Greeks glorified heroism and the Egyptians emphasized the eternal cycle of life and death, the Norse embraced the stark reality of fate and the inevitability of destruction.

In Greek mythology, gods like **Zeus** and **Hades** wield immense power over the heavens and the underworld, while the Egyptians honored **Ra** and **Osiris** as rulers of life and death. Similarly, the Norse gods like **Odin**, the seeker of wisdom, and **Thor**, the protector of Midgard, hold dominion over both divine realms and human affairs. But unlike the Greek gods, who are often depicted as capricious rulers, or the Egyptian gods, who maintain cosmic order, the Norse gods face an unyielding future: **Ragnarok**, the final battle, looms over them, a reminder that even gods are bound by fate.

The connection between **Greek, Egyptian,** and **Norse myths** also extends to their heroes and creatures. The Greeks had **Heracles**, the Egyptians had their mighty **pharaohs**, and the

Norse revered **Sigurd** and **Ragnar**—all legendary figures who crossed the line between mortal and divine. Similarly, the **monsters** of each mythos reflect the fears of their respective cultures: the **Hydra** and **Cerberus** in Greek mythology, the **Sphinx** and **Ammit** in Egyptian myth, and the fearsome **Fenrir** and **Jormungandr** in Norse tales. Each of these creatures represents chaos, death, and the wild forces of nature that gods and heroes must confront.

However, while the Greeks saw the potential for triumph over chaos and the Egyptians believed in an eternal afterlife, the Norse outlook was more somber. Fate, in Norse mythology, is inescapable. Even the greatest gods and heroes are destined to fall in **Ragnarok**, and yet, they face this fate with unmatched courage. The Norse sagas, like their Greek and Egyptian counterparts, are about the eternal struggle between order and chaos, but they also emphasize the bravery to face inevitable defeat with honor.

As you move through this book, you'll see how these Norse legends echo the themes of **Greek and Egyptian myths**, while bringing a unique perspective that is both heroic and poignant. From the love stories and tragedies to the cosmic battles that shake the heavens, the myths of these ancient cultures are all connected, offering insights into how humans across time have grappled with the forces that shape their world.

CHAPTER 1:
THE ORIGINS OF THE NORSE GODS

1.1 CREATION MYTHS OF NORSE COSMOLOGY

Ymir and the Primal Void of Ginnungagap

In the beginning, before the world as we know it existed, there was only the yawning void of **Ginnungagap**. This vast, empty chasm lay between two contrasting realms: to the north was **Niflheim**, a world of icy mists, frozen winds, and unending darkness; to the south was **Muspelheim**, a land of blistering heat and raging fires. These two realms were the source of the first forces of creation, where fire and ice would meet, and from their interaction, life would begin to stir.

As the icy rivers of Niflheim flowed southward, they collided with the fiery streams of Muspelheim. In the heart of Ginnungagap, the ice began to melt, and from this union of opposites, the **first giant, Ymir**, was born. Ymir was a primordial being, neither fully god nor mortal, but a creature of chaos and raw power. From Ymir's body, other giants emerged, growing from the sweat of his flesh, marking the beginning of the **Jotnar**, or giants, who would forever stand in opposition to the gods.

The Birth of the World from Ymir's Body

As Ymir slept, the cosmos slowly began to take shape. Alongside Ymir, the giant cow **Audhumla** was created from the melting ice. Audhumla's milk provided sustenance for Ymir, and as she licked the salty ice, she uncovered another figure: **Buri**, the ancestor of the gods. From Buri's descendants came **Odin**, **Vili**, and **Ve**, the first of the Aesir gods. These three brothers, recognizing that Ymir's chaotic nature posed a threat to the new world they wished to build, made a bold decision—they would slay Ymir and use his body to construct the cosmos.

In a titanic struggle, Odin and his brothers overcame Ymir, and from his colossal corpse, they fashioned the world. Ymir's **flesh** became the land, his **blood** the oceans and rivers, and his **bones** the mountains. His **skull** was lifted to form the sky, and his **brains** were scattered to create the clouds. The gods then placed **sparks** from Muspelheim in the sky, igniting the stars that would light the night.

With Ymir's death, the world as the Norse knew it took form. **Midgard**, the realm of humans, was shaped from Ymir's remains and placed at the center of the newly created universe. To protect Midgard from the giants, the gods fashioned a great barrier using Ymir's eyelashes. Around Midgard, other realms took shape, including **Asgard**, the home of the gods, and **Jotunheim**, the land of the giants, each bound by fate and destiny to the world formed from Ymir's sacrifice.

Cultural Impact and Legacy

The myth of Ymir's creation from Ginnungagap and the birth of the world from his body is central to Norse cosmology. It encapsulates the Norse belief in the cycle of creation and destruction, as well as the dual forces of chaos and order that govern the universe. Ymir, as a figure of chaos, reflects the untamed, wild nature of the world before the gods established order. His death, while violent, was a necessary sacrifice to bring structure to the cosmos, symbolizing the Norse understanding that creation often requires destruction.

This myth also highlights the Norse view of fate—an unavoidable force that even the gods must contend with. The shaping of the world from Ymir's body sets the stage for the eventual end of the cosmos in **Ragnarok**, a fate the gods themselves cannot escape. In this way, the myth of Ymir not only explains the creation of the physical world but also reflects the deeper, cyclical nature of existence in Norse mythology, where beginnings and endings are inextricably linked.

As you explore further into the myths of the Norse gods, heroes, and creatures, you will see how this primal act of creation ripples throughout their stories, from the shaping of Midgard to the eventual fall of the gods. The legacy of Ymir's body continues to define the structure of the cosmos and the eternal struggle between the forces of chaos and order.

1.2 THE YGGDRASIL: THE WORLD TREE

At the heart of Norse cosmology stands **Yggdrasil**, the great **World Tree**, a massive ash tree whose branches and roots stretch across the entire cosmos. Yggdrasil is not just a symbol of life but the very structure that holds together the Nine Realms of existence. The tree's mighty trunk serves as the axis that binds the heavens, the earth, and the underworld, linking gods, mortals, giants, and other creatures in an intricate web of fate.

Yggdrasil is described as **evergreen**, its leaves vibrant and eternal, signifying the interconnectedness of all life, death, and rebirth within the Norse universe. The tree's roots extend into the deepest realms, while its branches stretch high into the heavens, reaching toward the abode of the gods, **Asgard**. Its significance goes beyond just being a physical structure; it is a **sacred entity** that influences the fates of gods and mortals alike.

The World Tree as the Center of the Cosmos

In Norse mythology, Yggdrasil is the **center of the cosmos**, holding the Nine Realms in balance. These realms are not just physical spaces but represent the different aspects of existence—both seen and unseen. At the topmost branches lies **Asgard**, home of the Aesir gods, including Odin and Thor, where they oversee the fates of men and gods alike. Below Asgard is **Midgard**, the realm of humans, surrounded by a protective barrier, and connected to Asgard by the **Bifrost**, the rainbow bridge guarded by **Heimdall**.

Beneath the tree's roots lie the darker and more mysterious realms. **Helheim**, the land of the dead, ruled by the goddess **Hel**, resides in one of these deep, shadowy roots. Nearby is **Niflheim**, the icy world of mist and cold, from which the primordial forces of creation sprang. On the other side of the roots lies **Muspelheim**, the realm of fire, ruled by the giant **Surtr**, whose flames will one day ignite Ragnarok, the end of the world.

The World Tree's roots also extend into **Jotunheim**, the land of the giants, eternal enemies of the gods, and **Vanaheim**, the home of the Vanir gods, who govern nature and fertility. These realms, though distinct, are all part of the cosmic balance Yggdrasil maintains. Without the tree, the Nine Realms would fall into chaos, and the forces that bind the universe together would unravel.

Yggdrasil's Mystical Significance

More than just a physical link between realms, Yggdrasil is imbued with profound **mystical significance**. It is said that **Odin** himself hung from its branches for nine days and nights, sacrificing himself to gain the wisdom of the **runes**, the magical alphabet that governs fate and destiny. Through this act, Odin not only gained unparalleled knowledge but also symbolized the tree's role as a gateway to deeper wisdom and insight into the mysteries of existence.

Yggdrasil is also home to several creatures that play important roles in maintaining the cosmic balance. At the base of the tree resides **Nidhogg**, a dragon who gnaws at its roots, constantly threatening to bring destruction to the cosmos. High in the branches lives an eagle, whose sharp sight surveys the Nine Realms, and between them scurries **Ratatoskr**, a mischievous squirrel who carries messages of malice between the two creatures, further stirring the tension that underscores the precarious balance Yggdrasil represents.

At the well of **Urd**, located at one of the tree's roots, sit the **Norns**, three powerful beings who weave the threads of fate for all gods and mortals. Their presence at Yggdrasil's base underscores the tree's connection to fate and time, as they continually measure and cut the threads of life, determining the destiny of every being.

Symbolism and Cultural Impact

Yggdrasil stands as one of the most important symbols in Norse mythology, representing not only the structure of the universe but also the interconnectedness of all life and the unavoidable force of fate. It embodies the Norse belief in a **cyclical** universe, where life, death, and rebirth are in constant motion. The health of Yggdrasil reflects the state of the cosmos: as its roots are attacked by Nidhogg and other dark forces, the tree itself begins to wither, symbolizing the gradual decline of the world toward **Ragnarok**.

The World Tree also represents the **fragility** of balance in the universe. Even though it holds the Nine Realms together, it is constantly under threat, a reminder that chaos is always at the edges of order, waiting for a chance to strike. This fragility is mirrored in the lives of the gods and mortals, who must constantly fight to maintain harmony, knowing full well that fate will ultimately have its way.

In the culture of the Norse people, Yggdrasil was more than a mythological concept—it was a **spiritual framework** that helped them make sense of their world, their relationship with the gods, and the natural forces that surrounded them. It taught them that life was fleeting, that struggles were part of existence, and that the ultimate fate of the world was beyond anyone's control, even that of the gods themselves. Through Yggdrasil, the Norse embraced the inevitability of change, the interconnectedness of all things, and the eternal cycles that define existence.

In the vast expanse of Norse mythology, **giants**, known as the **Jotun** or **Jotnar**, play a pivotal role as agents of chaos and disorder. Far from mere antagonists, the giants represent primal forces that predate even the gods, embodying the wild, untamed elements of nature. While the gods, particularly the Aesir led by Odin, strive to maintain order and protect the cosmos, the giants are constant challengers, forever seeking to disrupt the balance and return the world to its chaotic origins.

The Antagonistic Role of the Giants

The giants, or Jotun, were among the first beings in existence, emerging from the primal void of **Ginnungagap**. As we have seen, the first giant, **Ymir**, was the source of all creation. But unlike the gods, who seek order and stability, the giants embody the wild, destructive forces that threaten to undo the cosmos. They hail from **Jotunheim**, one of the Nine Realms, a land of harsh wilderness, frozen mountains, and vast forests, mirroring their own untamed and unpredictable nature.

The giants are not merely enemies of the gods; they are forces of **nature** itself. Their colossal size and strength represent the raw power of the world—earthquakes, storms, and other uncontrollable phenomena that can reshape the world in an instant. While the gods seek to maintain **Ma'at**—the balance and order of the universe—the giants are agents of **chaos**, always challenging this balance, sometimes through direct conflict, and other times through cunning manipulation.

Cosmic Battles Between Gods and Giants

The relationship between the gods and the giants is complex and often contradictory. Though they are sworn enemies, locked in an eternal struggle, they are also intertwined through family ties and uneasy alliances. **Loki**, the trickster god, himself born of giants, embodies this duality. He is both a friend and an enemy to the Aesir, playing a key role in many of their victories but ultimately destined to betray them at **Ragnarok**.

One of the most famous conflicts between the gods and giants is the battle between **Thor** and the giant **Hrungnir**. Hrungnir, known for his immense strength, challenged Thor, the protector of both Midgard and Asgard, to a duel. In this cosmic clash, Thor's mighty hammer, **Mjolnir**, proved to be the instrument that not only defeated Hrungnir but also reaffirmed the gods' role as the protectors of the cosmos. This struggle between Thor and Hrungnir symbolizes the broader conflict between the forces of order (represented by the gods) and chaos (embodied by the giants).

Yet, despite these battles, the giants are not always depicted as purely evil. They are more accurately seen as necessary opposites to the gods, representing the **forces of nature** that are both feared and respected. While Thor's victories over giants like Hrungnir show the gods' ability to hold chaos at bay, these battles are never final. The giants will always return, just as the destructive forces of nature are ever-present in the lives of mortals.

This constant struggle between gods and giants mirrors the Norse worldview, where life is seen as a battle against uncontrollable forces. The gods are tasked with keeping these forces in check, but the Norse believed that such a struggle could never be truly won—only delayed.

Ragnarok and the Final Battle

The giants play a key role in **Ragnarok**, the foretold end of the world in Norse mythology. At this apocalyptic moment, the giants will rise up in one final, cataclysmic battle against the gods. Led by the fire giant **Surtr**, who comes from **Muspelheim**, the giants will storm **Asgard**, and Surtr's flaming sword will set the world ablaze, destroying everything in its path. Even **Odin** and **Thor**, the most powerful of the gods, are fated to fall during Ragnarok. Odin will be devoured by the monstrous wolf **Fenrir**, a creature born of giant heritage, while Thor will meet his end battling the **World Serpent**, **Jormungandr**, a giant serpent that encircles the earth.

In this final battle, the giants represent the ultimate chaos—the inevitable destruction of the world. Yet, just as Ymir's body was used to create the cosmos, from the ashes of Ragnarok, a new world will rise. The role of the giants, though destructive, is also **cyclical**, marking the end of one era and the beginning of another. Their constant presence serves as a reminder that chaos is not something to be defeated but something that exists in balance with order, a key element in the cycles of creation and destruction.

Symbolism and Cultural Impact

The giants in Norse mythology symbolize the uncontrollable forces of nature, the elements of chaos that constantly threaten to dismantle the order of the world. Through their battles with the gods, they embody the tension between creation and destruction, stability and disorder, that is central to the Norse understanding of existence. Just as the sea cannot be tamed, nor the storms halted, the giants represent the ever-present reminder that chaos is a necessary part of the cosmic order.

In the lives of the ancient Norse people, these myths reflected the **harsh realities** of their world. Living in a land of extreme weather and rugged landscapes, they understood that nature was both a provider and a destroyer, much like the giants themselves. These stories served to explain the uncontrollable forces around them, offering both a sense of awe and a reminder of the **fragility** of life.

Through the giants, the Norse saw that no victory was ever permanent and that even the gods were not immune to the forces of chaos. The ever-looming presence of Ragnarok further reinforced the idea that everything, even the gods, must one day fall to the inevitable cycle of creation and destruction. In this way, the giants and their role in Norse mythology remind us that chaos and order are two sides of the same coin, and it is through their eternal struggle that the world is shaped.

1.4 SUMMARY AND KEY TAKEAWAYS

Summary

In this chapter, we explored the foundational myths of Norse cosmology, focusing on the creation of the universe, the World Tree, and the eternal conflict between the gods and the giants. The **primal void of Ginnungagap** served as the stage for the collision of fire and ice, which gave birth to **Ymir**, the first giant. From his body, the gods—led by **Odin**—crafted the physical world, establishing order out of chaos.

We also encountered **Yggdrasil**, the mighty **World Tree** that holds the Nine Realms together, acting as a bridge between the heavens, earth, and the underworld. The tree's roots and branches bind the realms, linking **Asgard**, **Midgard**, and the darker regions like **Helheim**. Yggdrasil symbolizes the interconnectedness of all life and the cyclical nature of existence in Norse belief.

Finally, we delved into the antagonistic role of the **Jotun**, the giants, who represent the chaotic forces that challenge the gods. Their eternal struggle against the Aesir culminates in the final battle of **Ragnarok**, where the giants will rise again, reflecting the Norse acceptance of fate and the inevitable return of chaos.

Key Takeaways:

1. **Creation from Chaos**: The Norse cosmos was born from the meeting of fire and ice, with the giant Ymir representing primal chaos. His body became the foundation for the universe, showing the cyclical nature of creation and destruction in Norse belief.

2. **Yggdrasil as the Axis of the Universe**: The World Tree, Yggdrasil, serves as the central structure that holds the Nine Realms together, symbolizing the interconnectedness of life and the balance between order and chaos. Its roots and

branches link all beings—gods, mortals, and mythical creatures.

3. **The Giants as Forces of Chaos**: The Jotun, or giants, represent the untamed, destructive forces of nature and fate. Though they oppose the gods, they are an essential part of the cosmic order, ensuring the balance between creation and destruction.

4. **Fate and Ragnarok**: The inevitability of Ragnarok underscores the Norse understanding that fate governs all, even the gods. The giants' role in this final battle emphasizes the cyclical destruction and rebirth of the world, an unavoidable aspect of existence in Norse cosmology.

As you move forward, these themes of creation, balance, and fate will continue to shape the myths and stories of the gods, heroes, and creatures that inhabit the Norse universe. The battle between order and chaos is ever-present, influencing the lives of both gods and mortals alike.

Reflective Questions

- How does the Norse concept of creation from chaos, represented by the death of Ymir, reflect the Viking understanding of the balance between destruction and creation in their worldview?
- In what ways does Yggdrasil, the World Tree, symbolize the interconnectedness of life and fate across the Nine Realms? How does its role as the cosmic axis influence the actions of gods, giants, and mortals?
- What do the battles between the gods and the giants reveal about the Norse view of chaos and order? How does this eternal conflict shape the understanding of fate, especially in the lead-up to Ragnarok?

1.5 MYTHOLOGY QUIZ 1

Test your knowledge about the myths in Norse cosmology with the following questions:

1. **What was the name of the void that existed before the world was created?**

   A) Muspelheim

   B) Yggdrasil

   C) Ginnungagap

   D) Midgard

2. **Which two realms collided to create the conditions for life to begin?**

   A) Asgard and Jotunheim

   B) Muspelheim and Niflheim

   C) Midgard and Vanaheim

   D) Helheim and Alfheim

3. **Who was the first giant from whom the world was created?**

   A) Odin

   B) Fenrir

   C) Ymir

   D) Thor

4. **What did the gods use Ymir's skull to create?**

   A) The sea

   B) The sky

   C) The mountains

   D) The trees

5. **What is the name of the World Tree that connects the Nine Realms?**

   A) Ratatoskr

   B) Mjolnir

   C) Yggdrasil

   D) Nidhogg

6. **Which creature gnaws at the roots of Yggdrasil, threatening the tree's stability?**

   A) Fenrir

   B) Nidhogg

   C) Jormungandr

   D) Hrungnir

7. **What realm is the home of the giants?**

        A) Midgard

        B) Asgard

        C) Vanaheim

        D) Jotunheim

Note: Answers to the quiz can be found in the "Answer Key" section in the Appendix.

CHAPTER 2:
THE NINE REALMS OF NORSE COSMOLOGY

2.1 ASGARD: THE REALM OF THE GODS

At the very heart of Norse mythology lies **Asgard**, the majestic realm of the **Aesir**, the primary gods of the Norse pantheon. Often described as a mighty fortress surrounded by towering walls, Asgard is home to **Odin, Thor, Freyja**, and many other powerful gods. It is the center of divine power, where the gods rule over the cosmos, making decisions that affect not only their own realm but also the mortal world, **Midgard**, and the other realms of the Norse universe.

Asgard is connected to Midgard by the **Bifrost**, the rainbow bridge that stretches between the two worlds. The **Bifrost** is guarded by **Heimdall**, the ever-vigilant god with extraordinary senses, whose task is to protect Asgard from invaders and to sound the horn at the onset of **Ragnarok**, the prophesied end of the world. The connection between Asgard and Midgard is not just physical, but also symbolic of the relationship between gods and humans—the gods watch over and interact with the mortal world from their lofty perch.

Odin's Hall: Valhalla

Within Asgard lies **Valhalla**, Odin's great hall of the slain. It is here that the **Einherjar**, the spirits of warriors who died bravely in battle, reside. Chosen by the **Valkyries**, these warriors spend their days in combat, preparing for the final battle at Ragnarok, when they will fight alongside the gods. Valhalla is more than just a resting place for warriors; it is a symbol of the **Viking ethos**—valor in life and honor in death.

Fólkvangr: Freyja's Hall

While Valhalla is often the most celebrated part of Asgard, it is important to note that not all fallen warriors go to Odin's hall. Many are taken to **Fólkvangr**, the domain of **Freyja**, the goddess of love, war, and fertility. Freyja shares in the selection of the honored dead, and her hall is another place of glory for those who have shown exceptional bravery.

The Power and Politics of Asgard

Asgard is also the political center of the gods. Odin, known as the **Allfather**, presides over **The Thing**, the assembly of the gods, where important decisions are made. Odin's hall, **Valaskjalf**, with its high throne, **Hlidskjalf**, is where Odin watches over the entire cosmos, contemplating the fate of gods and mortals alike. It is here that Odin sacrifices for wisdom, constantly seeking knowledge, even at great personal cost, such as when he sacrifices an eye at **Mimir's Well** to gain insight into the mysteries of the universe.

The gods of Asgard are not infallible, nor are they free from conflict. The dynamics within Asgard are complex, with gods like **Loki**, the trickster, often causing trouble and strife. Though he resides among the Aesir, Loki's actions, driven by both malice and mischief, frequently disrupt the order of Asgard, setting in motion events that will eventually lead to Ragnarok.

The Role of Asgard in the Cosmic Balance

Asgard, despite its grandeur, is not eternal. The prophecies of Ragnarok suggest that Asgard will fall during the final battle, and many of the gods will perish in the flames of chaos. Yet, even in its destruction, Asgard represents the **cycle of death and rebirth** that defines the Norse worldview. Just as the gods prepare for the inevitable conflict, they also understand that the world will be reborn, and a new Asgard may rise from the ashes.

In Norse cosmology, Asgard is more than just a divine residence—it is the embodiment of **order, power, and fate**. It stands at the pinnacle of the Nine Realms, connected to them all but existing above them in both status and influence. The gods who live there hold sway over the cosmos, but they are also bound by the same inescapable fate that governs all things. Asgard's ultimate destiny is intertwined with the fate of the world, making it a key part of the Norse understanding of existence.

Cultural Impact

The image of Asgard as a mighty realm of gods has inspired countless interpretations in modern literature, art, and popular culture. From the **Marvel Cinematic Universe's** depiction of Asgard as a futuristic realm to the poetic descriptions found in the **Poetic Edda**, Asgard continues to captivate the imagination. Its themes of **heroism, sacrifice, and inevitable destiny** resonate deeply with audiences, ensuring that Asgard remains one of the most iconic symbols in Norse mythology.

2.2 MIDGARD: THE WORLD OF HUMANS

Midgard, the realm of humans, lies at the center of the Norse cosmological map, nestled between the divine Asgard and the more dangerous outer realms. The name itself means "middle enclosure" or "middle world," symbolizing its position as the central point of the cosmos, surrounded by the more mystical and perilous worlds of gods, giants, and creatures. Midgard is the place where the everyday dramas of life unfold—birth, death, love, war, and survival—all under the watchful eye of the gods.

Creation of Midgard

Midgard was created from the body of the **giant Ymir**, whose flesh, blood, and bones were used to form the world. According to the creation myths, the **Aesir** gods, led by **Odin**, constructed Midgard as a safe haven for humans, protected from the chaos that exists in the surrounding realms. The walls of Midgard were built from Ymir's eyebrows to shield humanity from the dangers of the outside world, especially the **Jotun**, the giants who resided in **Jotunheim**.

This creation story underscores the Norse belief that humanity is both part of the cosmic order and subject to the whims of divine and chaotic forces. The fact that Midgard was shaped from the remains of a chaotic giant illustrates the precarious balance between order and chaos in the Norse worldview.

Humans in Midgard

In Midgard, humans live out their lives, often unaware of the larger cosmic struggles that influence their existence. However, the gods are always watching over them, intervening at key moments, or offering guidance through signs, dreams, and omens. **Odin**, in particular, is known for his involvement in the affairs of men, often disguising himself to walk among them, gathering wisdom and testing the courage of warriors.

For the Norse people, the idea of fate, or **wyrd**, played a central role in human life. The **Norns**, the weavers of fate, controlled the destiny of both gods and men, and their decisions were final. Although humans in Midgard had the ability to make choices, their ultimate fate was already woven into the fabric of existence. This concept of fate resonated deeply with the Viking ethos, where bravery and honor in the face of inevitable death were prized above all else.

Midgard's Connection to the Other Realms

The most significant connection between Midgard and the other realms is the **Bifrost**, the rainbow bridge that links it to **Asgard**. This bridge serves as a direct pathway for the gods to interact with humans, but it is also a symbol of the divine protection that shields Midgard from the chaos of the other realms.

While Midgard is relatively peaceful compared to the more chaotic realms like **Jotunheim** or **Muspelheim**, it is not entirely free from danger. Giants, dragons, and other mythical creatures occasionally make their way into Midgard, challenging the strength of human heroes and testing the resolve of mortal warriors. In these moments, human champions—armed with divine blessings or magical knowledge—are called upon to defend Midgard from these threats.

Midgard is also vulnerable to the larger cosmic events that affect all of the Nine Realms. The most notable of these is **Ragnarok**, the final battle that will see the end of many gods, and the destruction of Midgard itself. During Ragnarok, the world will be consumed by fire and chaos, and the seas will rise, drowning everything in their path. However, after this great destruction, it is said that Midgard will be reborn, purified and ready for a new age of peace and prosperity.

Midgard in Norse Mythology

In many of the **heroic sagas**, Midgard is where mortal heroes perform their feats of bravery and valor. Heroes such as **Sigurd**, who slayed the dragon **Fafnir**, and **Ragnar Lothbrok**, the legendary Viking chieftain, lived in Midgard and became renowned for their extraordinary deeds. These sagas highlight the important role humans played in the mythological landscape, demonstrating that even in a world filled with gods and giants, mortal courage and strength were equally celebrated.

Although Midgard is a realm of mortals, it is not a place of insignificance. The gods take great interest in the affairs of humans, and warriors who die bravely in battle are often chosen by the **Valkyries** to join the gods in **Valhalla**, where they prepare for the final battle. This strong connection between Midgard and Asgard illustrates the mutual dependence between gods and humans. The gods need brave mortals to join their ranks for Ragnarok, just as mortals rely on the gods for protection and guidance.

Cultural Impact

For the Norse people, Midgard was not just a mythological concept but a reflection of their own world. It represented the challenges and dangers they faced daily, from the natural elements to warfare, while also symbolizing the divine protection they believed was granted by the gods. The idea that their world was one part of a much larger cosmic structure made the Norse people acutely aware of their place in the universe, where fate and destiny played central roles.

In modern culture, Midgard has continued to be a powerful symbol, often used in literature, video games, and movies to represent the human world in fantasy settings. The concept of a realm where humans coexist with divine powers and supernatural forces has inspired countless adaptations, keeping the spirit of Norse mythology alive in popular imagination.

2.3 NIFLHEIM AND MUSPELHEIM: REALMS OF ICE AND FIRE

In Norse cosmology, the realms of **Niflheim** and **Muspelheim** represent the extreme forces of **cold and fire** that were instrumental in the creation of the world and continue to play crucial roles in its eventual destruction. These two realms are primal and elemental, standing in stark contrast to the more developed and inhabited worlds like **Asgard** and **Midgard**. As the forces of **ice and fire**, they are both the **origin and end** of existence, embodying the cycles of **creation and destruction** that run through Norse mythology.

Niflheim: The Realm of Ice

Niflheim is the realm of **ice, cold, and mist**, lying to the north of **Ginnungagap**, the primordial void. One of the oldest realms, Niflheim is a world of perpetual frost and darkness, where icy winds blow and freezing rivers flow endlessly. Its name translates to "Mist-Home," and it is often depicted as a desolate and inhospitable land, shrouded in **fog and frozen waters**. This cold, barren landscape contrasts sharply with the fiery nature of **Muspelheim**, symbolizing the balance between opposing forces in the Norse cosmos.

Niflheim is home to **Hvergelmir**, the spring from which the **Elivagar** rivers flow. These rivers of ice were among the first elements to exist in the cosmos and played a crucial role in the creation of the world. It was from the frozen waters of Niflheim that the first giant, **Ymir**, was formed. His creation set into motion the events that would eventually lead to the formation of Midgard and the other realms. Niflheim's ice, combined with the fiery heat from Muspelheim, gave birth to Ymir, whose body was used by the gods to create the world. This interplay between ice and fire is a recurring theme, representing the **tension between creation and destruction**.

Another significant part of Niflheim is **Helheim**, the underworld ruled by **Hel**, daughter of **Loki**. Though sometimes referred to interchangeably, Niflheim and Helheim are distinct regions. While Niflheim is the land of primordial ice, Helheim is where those who die of sickness or old age are sent. Helheim is dark and cold, mirroring Niflheim's bleak environment, and it is here that souls remain in a state of **eternal rest or punishment** under Hel's dominion.

Symbolism of Niflheim

Niflheim represents **death, coldness, and stillness**, and its presence in Norse mythology serves as a reminder of the **inevitability of death** and the **harsh realities of existence**. It is a realm of **stasis**, where nothing grows, and life is nearly impossible. This symbolizes the concept of **entropy**, the eventual freezing of all things, and the idea that life must constantly struggle against the forces of decay and stagnation.

Niflheim's role in the creation of the world is significant because it highlights the necessity of opposites. Without the ice of Niflheim, the world could not have been formed, and without its cold, the fires of Muspelheim would have no counterpart to create the balance necessary for life. In this way, Niflheim is both the source of life and the embodiment of death—a realm that encapsulates the **cyclical nature of existence**.

Muspelheim: The Realm of Fire

Directly opposing Niflheim is **Muspelheim**, the realm of **fire, heat, and chaos**. Located to the south of Ginnungagap, Muspelheim is a fiery, volcanic land where flames roar endlessly, and rivers of molten lava flow. It is ruled by the fire giant **Surtr**, who wields a **flaming sword** and plays a central role in the prophecy of **Ragnarok**, where he will lead the fire giants in a final, devastating assault on the gods and the cosmos.

Muspelheim's fire, like Niflheim's ice, is an elemental force of creation and destruction. The intense heat from Muspelheim met the cold of Niflheim in Ginnungagap, leading to the formation of **Ymir** and, ultimately, the creation of the Nine Realms. This meeting of extreme forces symbolizes the **birth of the universe** from chaos, a central theme in Norse cosmology. Without the heat of Muspelheim, the ice of Niflheim would remain stagnant, and without the ice, Muspelheim's fire would consume all.

Surtr and the Role of Fire Giants

Surtr, the ruler of Muspelheim, is one of the most powerful and feared beings in Norse mythology. His flaming sword is said to be so hot that it will burn the entire cosmos during **Ragnarok**, reducing everything to ash and paving the way for a new world to rise from the flames. The fire giants of Muspelheim are destructive forces, representing the uncontrollable, chaotic aspects of nature. Unlike the frost giants of **Jotunheim**, who are often depicted as a threat to the gods but still part of the cosmic balance, the fire giants are harbingers of destruction, playing a decisive role in the **apocalypse**.

Muspelheim itself is a hostile and dangerous place, where no living creature can survive except the fire giants and their kind. It is a realm of **pure destruction**, and its fire is not life-giving like the sun but rather life-consuming. This destructive energy is both feared and respected by the gods, who know that while they can stave off chaos for a time, they cannot stop the inevitable fires of Ragnarok.

Symbolism of Muspelheim

Muspelheim's fire represents **chaos, destruction, and renewal**. Just as fire can destroy forests but also clear the way for new growth, Muspelheim is both an end and a beginning. Its role in Ragnarok underscores this duality: while the flames of Surtr will bring about the end of the gods and the world as it is known, it will also clear the path for the rebirth of the cosmos. In this sense, fire is not merely destructive but also transformative—a necessary force for **change** and **renewal**.

Muspelheim's opposition to Niflheim reflects the Norse understanding of the world as a place of constant **conflict between opposing forces**. These forces are not inherently evil or good but are part of the natural order, contributing to the balance of the universe. Muspelheim's fire is a reminder that destruction is a necessary precursor to creation, and that from the ashes of the old, new life will eventually emerge.

The Interplay of Niflheim and Muspelheim

Together, Niflheim and Muspelheim represent the two extremes of existence—**ice and fire**, **stasis and chaos**, **death and destruction**. They are the elemental forces that shaped the universe at its beginning and will be the forces that bring it to an end at Ragnarok. These realms exist in stark contrast to Midgard and Asgard, where life thrives, but they are essential to the cosmic balance. Without the cold of Niflheim, the fires of Muspelheim would consume everything unchecked, and without the fire, Niflheim would be a realm of eternal stillness. Their opposition creates the tension necessary for the world's existence.

Cultural Impact

Niflheim and Muspelheim's imagery has been a source of fascination for modern storytellers and artists. The clash of ice and fire is a recurring motif in literature, film, and fantasy, often symbolizing the struggle between opposing forces of creation and destruction. In works like **George R.R. Martin's** *A Song of Ice and Fire*, the concept of two elemental forces locked in eternal conflict reflects this ancient Norse cosmological idea. In modern adaptations of Norse mythology, such as **Marvel's Thor**, the destructive power of Surtr and the fiery chaos of Muspelheim are brought vividly to life, showing how these ancient concepts continue to resonate in contemporary culture.

2.4 ALFHEIM AND SVARTALFHEIM: REALMS OF ELVES AND DWARVES

In Norse mythology, **Alfheim** and **Svartalfheim** are realms inhabited by two distinct groups of magical beings—the **elves** and the **dwarves**. These realms, while not as central to the cosmology as Asgard or Midgard, play crucial roles in the mythological framework, particularly through their association with **magic**, **craftsmanship**, and **fate**. The beings who dwell in these realms often interact with the gods, providing them with tools, weapons, and even assistance in their cosmic struggles.

Alfheim: The Realm of the Light Elves

Alfheim is the realm of the **light elves**, a race of ethereal beings who are described as **radiant** and **beautiful**. The elves of Alfheim are often associated with **light** and **magic**, and they are thought to possess powers beyond those of mortals, though they are not gods. Alfheim is ruled by **Frey**, one of the **Vanir** gods who is closely associated with **fertility**, **prosperity**, and **nature**. The light elves are thought to be benevolent creatures, bringing blessings to the human world, and in some accounts, they are seen as protectors of nature and the earth's bounty.

Though not much is written about Alfheim in the surviving Norse texts, the light elves are often seen as intermediaries between the gods and humans. Their world is one of light and purity, contrasting with the more subterranean and dark nature of the dwarves in **Svartalfheim**. In some stories, the elves are described as almost **angelic** beings, often linked to the forces of **life and growth**, which is fitting given their connection to Frey.

Elves also play a role in **healing** and **protection**. They are sometimes invoked in rituals to help with illness or to provide blessings for crops and families. This association with **fertility** and **abundance** further solidifies their role in maintaining the **balance of nature**. While they do not feature as prominently as the gods or giants in many myths, the elves' role as magical beings capable of influencing the natural world makes them important figures in the overall mythological landscape.

Svartalfheim: The Realm of the Dwarves

In stark contrast to the light and magic of Alfheim, **Svartalfheim** is the dark, subterranean world of the **dwarves**, also known as **dark elves** or **Svartálfar**. The dwarves of Svartalfheim are master craftsmen, known for their extraordinary skills in **forging weapons**, **tools**, and **magical artifacts**. While often described as small and sturdy beings, the dwarves wield great power through their craftsmanship, which has a significant impact on the fate of gods and mortals alike.

Some of the most famous objects in Norse mythology are created by the dwarves, including **Mjolnir**, Thor's hammer; **Gungnir**, Odin's spear; and **Draupnir**, Odin's magical ring. These artifacts are not merely weapons but are imbued with magical properties that reflect the skill and knowledge of the dwarves. Their ability to craft such powerful items underscores the importance of **artisanship and skill** in the Norse worldview—great power often comes not from brute strength but from the ability to shape and mold the world through craftsmanship.

The dwarves are also linked to the **underground**, which aligns them with the forces of the **earth** and its hidden powers. They live in **caves** and **forges** deep within the earth, often isolated from the other realms, focusing on their work. Despite their isolation, their influence is felt across the Nine Realms, as the objects they create often play pivotal roles in the myths. For example, **Loki**, in one of his many misadventures, manipulates the dwarves into crafting several of these legendary items, setting in motion events that will affect both gods and giants.

While the dwarves are generally seen as **neutral** figures, focused on their craft rather than the cosmic struggles between gods and giants, they are not above mischief or greed. In some stories, they are depicted as being driven by the desire for **wealth** and **power**, hoarding gold and jewels in their underground homes. This gives them a more ambiguous role in Norse mythology, where they can be both helpful and dangerous, depending on the situation.

Alfheim and Svartalfheim in the Cosmic Balance

The realms of **Alfheim** and **Svartalfheim** represent the **dual aspects of magic** and **craftsmanship** in Norse mythology. While the elves of Alfheim are linked to the forces of **light** and **life**, the dwarves of Svartalfheim are tied to the more practical, material aspects of creation. Together, they illustrate the Norse belief that both the **spiritual** and **material** worlds are important in maintaining balance.

The gods, particularly **Odin** and **Thor**, often rely on the dwarves for their skill in crafting the tools that will help them in their cosmic battles. Similarly, the blessings of the elves are sought for protection, healing, and prosperity. These realms, though not as well-known as Asgard or Midgard, play vital roles in ensuring the gods have what they need to protect the Nine Realms and keep chaos at bay.

The interaction between the gods and the inhabitants of these realms shows the **interconnectedness** of all beings in Norse cosmology. Even though the elves and dwarves exist in worlds separate from Asgard, Midgard, and Jotunheim, their actions and creations have a profound impact on the fate of the gods and humans. This highlights the Norse belief that **every realm and every being** plays a part in the greater cosmic story.

Cultural Impact

The concept of elves and dwarves has had a lasting influence on modern fantasy literature and popular culture. Elves, often depicted as graceful, wise, and magical beings, and dwarves, known for their strength, endurance, and craftsmanship, have become staples of the **fantasy genre**, appearing in works like **J.R.R. Tolkien's** *The Lord of the Rings* and countless other books, films, and games. The imagery of the elves as protectors of nature and the dwarves as master smiths can be traced back to their origins in Norse mythology, where these beings played essential roles in shaping the world.

2.5 JOTUNHEIM: LAND OF THE GIANTS

In Norse mythology, **Jotunheim** is the realm of the **Jotnar**, also known as **giants**. This vast, wild land lies in stark contrast to the ordered, divine realm of **Asgard**. Jotunheim is a place of **chaos**, **untamed nature**, and **hostility**, ruled by these powerful and often antagonistic beings. While the giants are seen as forces of destruction and disorder, their presence in Norse cosmology is essential, embodying the natural forces that constantly threaten the balance of the cosmos.

Jotunheim is located far from the orderly worlds of gods and men. It is separated from Midgard by the **Elivagar** rivers, a series of impassable waters that serve as a barrier between the giants and humans. The giants are the ancient enemies of the **Aesir**, the gods who reside in Asgard, and many of the myths center around the constant struggles between these two powerful groups. Despite this enmity, there is also a strange interdependence between the gods and giants, making Jotunheim a realm of complexity and contradiction.

The Giants of Jotunheim

The giants of Jotunheim are not mere brute monsters, though they are often portrayed as immense in size and strength. They are deeply connected to the forces of **nature**, particularly the untamed aspects like storms, frost, and mountains. In fact, there are different types of giants: the **frost giants**, associated with cold and ice, and the **fire giants**, linked to the destructive power of fire (though the fire giants reside in **Muspelheim**, not Jotunheim).

While many giants are antagonists in Norse myths, some display **wisdom and foresight** that even the gods respect. For example, the giantess **Skadi** marries the sea god **Njord**, becoming one of the Aesir. Giants are also known for their knowledge of **magic** and **prophecy**, making them more than just foes for the gods to conquer. The complex nature of the giants suggests that they represent the **unpredictable** and **dual-sided** nature of the world—they can bring both destruction and wisdom.

One of the most famous giants is **Ymir**, the primordial being whose body was used to create the world. Ymir's death at the hands of Odin and his brothers symbolizes the triumph of **order** over **chaos**, but it also shows the reliance of the gods on the primal forces represented by the giants. Even after Ymir's death, the giants continue to play a vital role in maintaining the cosmic balance, acting as the opposition that challenges the gods.

Utgard: The Stronghold of the Giants

Within Jotunheim lies **Utgard**, the stronghold of the giants, ruled by the powerful giant **Utgard-Loki** (not to be confused with **Loki**, the trickster god). Utgard is a place of illusion, trickery, and immense power, where the rules of reality seem to bend. One of the most famous myths involving Utgard-Loki is when **Thor** and **Loki** travel to Jotunheim and encounter a series of illusions that challenge their strength and intelligence. Though Thor's immense power is on display, the giants use trickery to humble him, showing that brute strength alone cannot overcome the forces of chaos.

Utgard represents the **mind-bending** and **unpredictable nature** of Jotunheim. Unlike the structured halls of Asgard, where rules and order govern all things, Utgard is a place where nothing is as it seems. The giants' ability to manipulate their environment and their connection to both natural and supernatural forces make Jotunheim a realm of danger and mystery.

The Giants' Role in Ragnarok

Though the gods and giants are locked in an eternal struggle, it is the giants who will play a decisive role in the destruction of the world during **Ragnarok**. Led by **Surtr**, the fire giant, the giants will storm Asgard, breaking through the defenses and initiating the final battle. **Loki**, the trickster god who straddles the line between the gods and giants, will also side with the giants in this conflict, leading to the downfall of many of the Aesir.

The giants' role in Ragnarok underscores their position as the **agents of chaos and destruction**. However, it is important to remember that in Norse mythology, destruction is not seen as purely negative—it is a necessary part of the cosmic cycle. The giants' victory in Ragnarok will pave the way for a **new world** to be born from the ashes of the old one. This cyclical view of time means that even though the giants bring about destruction, they also enable **renewal** and **rebirth**.

Relations Between Gods and Giants

While the gods and giants are often enemies, there is also a curious relationship between them. Many gods have giant ancestry, blurring the lines between the two groups. **Loki**, the trickster god, is himself of giant descent, and his complex role in Norse mythology reflects the blurred boundaries between good and evil, order and chaos. **Thor**, the protector of Asgard and Midgard, is constantly at odds with the giants, yet he has a deep respect for their power.

In several myths, gods travel to Jotunheim either to seek wisdom or to confront the giants. These journeys often reveal the **limitations of the gods' power** and highlight the giants' ability to **influence fate**. The gods may rule the cosmos, but they are not invincible, and the giants serve as a reminder that chaos and destruction are always just beyond the horizon.

The interactions between gods and giants, whether in conflict or cooperation, highlight the **interconnectedness of all beings** in Norse mythology. The giants are not merely enemies to be vanquished; they are part of the cosmic order, representing forces that are necessary for the universe's balance.

Cultural Impact

The image of giants as formidable beings tied to the natural world has had a significant influence on modern fantasy literature and popular culture. In many fantasy works, giants are portrayed as towering creatures connected to the land, embodying the same untamed forces seen in Norse mythology. For example, in **J.R.R. Tolkien's** *The Hobbit* and *The Lord of the Rings*, giants appear as elemental forces tied to the mountains and earth, much like the frost and stone giants of Jotunheim. The idea of a **wild, dangerous realm** inhabited by primal beings continues to inspire stories of conflict between order and chaos, showing the lasting appeal of Jotunheim and its inhabitants.

2.6 VANAHEIM: HOME OF THE VANIR GODS

In Norse mythology, **Vanaheim** is the realm of the **Vanir**, a group of gods associated with **fertility, nature, wealth, and prosperity**. The Vanir are often seen as complementary to the **Aesir** gods, who rule over Asgard and are linked to **war, power, and governance**. While the Aesir are often portrayed as the dominant pantheon, the Vanir play an essential role in maintaining the balance of the cosmos, particularly through their connection to the natural world and the cycles of life.

Vanaheim is depicted as a lush and fertile land, reflecting the powers of the Vanir gods. It is a realm where the forces of **growth, renewal**, and **abundance** thrive, in contrast to the more militaristic and structured nature of Asgard. The Vanir are deeply connected to the earth, and their magic is often linked to the **fertility of the land**, the **blessings of harvests**, and the **protection of the natural world**.

The Vanir Gods

The Vanir are a distinct group of gods, although they eventually become integrated with the Aesir following a truce after the **Aesir-Vanir War**, one of the most important events in Norse mythology. The war between the Aesir and Vanir is said to have been caused by mutual distrust and the differences in their powers and domains. The **Aesir**, representing power and war, clashed with the **Vanir**, who embodied nature and fertility. After a prolonged conflict, a **truce** was established, leading to an exchange of gods to foster peace. This blending of pantheons symbolizes the reconciliation between two essential forces: the **natural**, life-giving aspects of the world and the **warrior-like, governing order**.

Among the most well-known Vanir gods are **Njord**, **Frey**, and **Freyja**. These gods embody the Vanir's connection to fertility, wealth, and the sea.

- **Njord**, the father of Frey and Freyja, is the god of the **sea**, **fishing**, and **seafaring**, representing the wealth and sustenance that the ocean provides. His role as a Vanir god highlights the importance of the sea as a source of life and prosperity, particularly for the Norse people, who relied heavily on the ocean for trade and sustenance.
- **Frey**, Njord's son, is one of the most important deities when it comes to **fertility**, **sunshine**, and **prosperity**. He is often associated with **peace**, **wealth**, and **bountiful harvests**. Frey's powers extend over the earth and its ability to provide for humans, ensuring that crops grow and livestock thrive. His marriage to the giantess **Gerd** is a symbol of the harmony between humans and nature, reflecting the Vanir's role in ensuring the **fertility** and **sustenance** of the world.
- **Freyja**, Frey's sister, is a complex figure who embodies both **love and beauty** as well as **war and death**. She is a goddess of **love, fertility, and magic**, and her mastery of **Seidr**, a form of Norse sorcery, makes her a powerful figure among the gods. Freyja's association with fertility extends to her role as a protector of life, while her connection to war comes through her leadership of the **Valkyries**, who select warriors to join her hall, **Fólkvangr**, after their deaths in battle. Freyja's dual nature as both a goddess of love and war makes her one of the most intriguing figures in Norse mythology.

The Aesir-Vanir War and Its Resolution

The war between the Aesir and Vanir was a pivotal moment in the relationship between the two pantheons. Though the conflict between them caused great destruction, its resolution through peace and the exchange of gods signified the **reconciliation between order and nature**, a central theme in Norse mythology. To maintain peace, the Vanir sent **Njord**, **Frey**, and **Freyja** to live among the Aesir, while the Aesir sent **Hoenir** and **Mimir** to live among the Vanir. This exchange not only brought about a balance between the two realms but also ensured that the powers of both the Vanir and Aesir would work together to maintain cosmic harmony.

The blending of the Aesir and Vanir can be seen as a metaphor for the need for **balance** between the forces of nature and the structured order of society. While the Aesir focus on governance, war, and power, the Vanir represent the **softer forces** of nature, fertility, and growth. This symbiotic relationship is essential to the survival of the cosmos, as one cannot exist without the other.

Vanaheim and Its Role in the Cosmic Balance

Though Vanaheim is not often as prominently featured in the myths as realms like Asgard or Midgard, its importance is clear. As the home of the Vanir, it represents the **life-giving** and **nurturing** aspects of the universe. The gods of Vanaheim are responsible for ensuring that the natural world thrives, that the earth remains fertile, and that peace and prosperity are maintained.

Vanaheim also embodies the **cyclical nature of life**, where growth and renewal are constant processes. The Vanir gods, through their connection to the cycles of nature, play a crucial role in ensuring the **continuation of life**, both for the gods and for humans. Their power is not one of domination but of **nurturing**, making them essential to the overall balance of the cosmos.

Cultural Impact

The Vanir gods' association with fertility, nature, and prosperity has influenced modern depictions of deities and magical beings linked to **growth, abundance**, and **the natural world**. The themes of peace and fertility, embodied by Frey and Freyja, continue to resonate in literature, art, and culture, reminding us of the importance of harmony with nature. Their role in balancing the Aesir's more warlike and structured nature has shaped how we view the forces that govern the universe—not only in Norse mythology but in the broader realm of myth and storytelling.

2.7 HELHEIM: THE REALM OF THE DEAD

Helheim, one of the Nine Realms, is the somber and cold realm ruled by **Hel**, the daughter of **Loki**. Unlike the glorious afterlife of **Valhalla**, where warriors who die bravely in battle are taken, Helheim is the destination for those who die of **old age**, **sickness**, or **natural causes**. It is a place of **stillness and shadow**, far removed from the light and vitality of the living realms.

Helheim lies beneath the roots of **Yggdrasil**, the World Tree, and is often depicted as a **dark, gloomy** realm where the dead reside in quiet solitude. There is no glory or heroism in

Helheim—just the **inevitability of death** and the cold, unchanging nature of the afterlife. The very word "Hel" is connected to both the realm and its ruler, signifying both the place of the dead and the goddess who watches over them.

Hel: The Goddess of the Underworld

Hel, the ruler of this shadowy realm, is one of the most intriguing and mysterious figures in Norse mythology. She is described as having a dual appearance—**half alive** and **half dead**, with one side of her body appearing healthy and the other decaying. This physical manifestation of life and death symbolizes her power over both realms and the **duality** of her nature.

Hel is often portrayed as **stern and uncompromising**, but she is not evil. She simply oversees the souls of those who are not chosen for Valhalla or **Fólkvangr**. Unlike her father, Loki, who is known for mischief and chaos, Hel's role is more solemn. She maintains the balance between life and death, ensuring that those who pass from the world of the living are received into her care.

Though Hel rules over the dead, she is not a figure of **punishment**. The souls that enter Helheim are not tortured or condemned in the same way as those in Christian conceptions of the underworld. Instead, they reside in a state of **eternal rest**, neither suffering nor experiencing joy. This neutrality reflects the Norse view of death as an **inevitable part of life**, rather than something to be feared or avoided.

The Road to Helheim

To reach Helheim, the souls of the dead must traverse a long and difficult path. The journey takes them over the **Gjallarbrú**, the bridge over the **Gjoll River**, which marks the boundary between the land of the living and the land of the dead. The bridge is guarded by **Modgud**, a giantess who allows only the dead to pass. This crossing is symbolic of the final separation between life and death, as once a soul has passed over the Gjallarbrú, there is no return to the living world.

Once in Helheim, souls are said to live in a **shadowy existence**, where time stands still. They no longer partake in the struggles or joys of life but remain in a passive state, disconnected from the activities of the living realms. Unlike Valhalla, where warriors spend their afterlife preparing for the final battle of **Ragnarok**, the dead in Helheim simply exist, awaiting their final fate when Ragnarok unfolds.

The Role of Helheim in Ragnarok

Though Helheim is a place of stillness, it plays a significant role in the events of **Ragnarok**, the Norse apocalypse. During Ragnarok, the souls of the dead in Helheim, led by Hel herself, will rise and join the forces of chaos in the battle against the gods. The dead, who were previously passive and inactive, will take up arms alongside **Loki** and **Surtr**, the fire giant, contributing to the destruction of the world.

This part of the prophecy underscores the Norse belief that death is an inescapable force. While the gods may be powerful, even they cannot prevent the dead from joining in the cosmic struggle that will ultimately end the world as it is known. Helheim, therefore, serves as a **reservoir of fate**, holding the dead until the day they will play their role in the ultimate destruction and rebirth of the cosmos.

Helheim's Contrast to Valhalla and Fólkvangr

Helheim's stark contrast to the afterlives of **Valhalla** and **Fólkvangr** is significant in Norse mythology. Valhalla, Odin's hall, is a place of glory, where warriors who die heroically are given the honor of feasting with the gods and preparing for the final battle of Ragnarok. Similarly, Fólkvangr, Freyja's realm, offers a place of honor for fallen warriors.

In contrast, Helheim is a place for those who die a more **mundane** death. There is no glory in Helheim, and the souls who reside there are not destined to fight in Ragnarok as the **Einherjar** of Valhalla are. This division between the honored dead and the rest reflects the Norse focus on **heroism** and **valor** as the highest virtues. To die in battle was to be remembered and celebrated, while to die of natural causes meant an unremarkable existence in the afterlife.

Yet, Helheim is not without dignity. It is a necessary part of the Norse cosmology, representing the reality of death for the majority of people. The souls in Helheim may not be honored as heroes, but they are not forgotten. They are part of the great cycle of life, death, and rebirth that governs the universe.

Cultural Impact

Helheim, and the figure of Hel herself, have influenced many modern interpretations of the afterlife, particularly in fantasy literature and media. The concept of a realm of the dead ruled by a mysterious figure has appeared in countless stories, from **J.R.R. Tolkien's** *The Lord of the Rings* to contemporary video games and films. Hel's dual nature as both life and death continues to captivate audiences, and the idea of a cold, shadowy afterlife echoes in various cultural depictions of the underworld. While Helheim is less glamorous than Valhalla, its quiet presence in the myths remains a powerful reminder of the inevitability of death and the mystery of what lies beyond life.

2.8 SUMMARY AND KEY TAKEAWAYS

Summary

In this chapter, we explored the diverse realms of Norse cosmology, each representing a unique aspect of existence, from the divine power of the gods to the forces of nature and death. These realms are not just settings for mythical tales but embodiments of the elements and concepts that govern the universe in Norse mythology.

Asgard: The Realm of the Gods

Asgard, home to the **Aesir gods**, stands as a bastion of divine power and order. The gods, led by **Odin**, protect the Nine Realms from the forces of chaos while preparing for **Ragnarok**, the inevitable end. **Valhalla**, Odin's hall for the heroic dead, and **Fólkvangr**, Freyja's domain, reflect the Norse belief in **valor** and **honor** in death.

Midgard: The World of Humans

Midgard, the realm of mortals, is central in the cosmology, representing the **human experience** of life, death, and fate. It is the battleground for heroism, where humans live under the protection of **Thor** and the watchful eye of the gods, while facing the inevitable threat of **chaos** from giants and other creatures.

Niflheim and Muspelheim: Realms of Ice and Fire

Niflheim, the realm of **ice** and **cold**, and Muspelheim, the realm of **fire**, are elemental forces at the heart of creation and destruction. These two realms embody the **duality of existence**, as the cold and heat from these worlds sparked the creation of the universe. Their opposing forces will ultimately collide during **Ragnarok**, bringing about the end of the world.

Alfheim and Svartalfheim: Realms of Elves and Dwarves

Alfheim, the land of the **light elves**, is a realm of beauty and **magic**, while **Svartalfheim**, home to the **dwarves**, is a world of **craftsmanship** and underground riches. The elves and dwarves play crucial roles in aiding the gods, providing **magical blessings** and forging legendary **weapons and tools** that influence the fate of the cosmos.

Jotunheim: Land of the Giants

Jotunheim is the realm of the **giants**, the eternal enemies of the gods, representing the forces of **chaos** and **destruction**. Though often at odds with the gods, the giants are also integral to the cosmic balance, providing a necessary challenge to the forces of order. The complex relationship between gods and giants highlights the **interconnectedness** of all beings in Norse mythology.

Vanaheim: Home of the Vanir Gods

Vanaheim, the land of the **Vanir gods**, is associated with **fertility**, **nature**, and **prosperity**. The Vanir, led by gods like **Frey**, **Freyja**, and **Njord**, balance the more warlike Aesir gods, ensuring the natural world continues to thrive. The **Aesir-Vanir War** and eventual truce symbolize the necessity of both **warrior strength** and **natural growth** for the cosmos to function harmoniously.

Helheim: The Realm of the Dead

Helheim, ruled by **Hel**, is the realm where those who die of old age or sickness dwell. Unlike Valhalla's glory, Helheim is a place of **eternal rest** without suffering or heroism. It plays a significant role during **Ragnarok**, when the dead will rise to fight alongside the forces of chaos, highlighting the Norse view of death as part of the cosmic cycle.

Key Takeaways:

1. **Cosmic Balance and Interconnection**
   The Nine Realms represent the intricate balance between **order** and **chaos**, **life** and **death**, and **growth** and **destruction**. Each realm plays a crucial role in maintaining the universe's structure, and the gods, giants, and other beings are all connected in this cosmic web.

2. **Fate and Heroism**
   Many realms reflect the Norse preoccupation with **fate** and **honor**. In realms like Asgard, Midgard, and Valhalla, **heroism** is celebrated, and those who die bravely are rewarded. In contrast, realms like Helheim remind us of the inevitability of death for all beings, regardless of glory.

3. **Creation and Destruction Cycles**
   Niflheim and Muspelheim embody the elemental forces that both create and destroy the universe. These cycles of **birth, destruction, and rebirth** are fundamental to Norse mythology, culminating in the prophecy of **Ragnarok**, where the realms will clash and lead to the world's renewal.

The Nine Realms, though vastly different, are bound by a shared fate, highlighting the complex and cyclical nature of Norse cosmology. From the glorious halls of Asgard to the shadowy depths of Helheim, the realms provide a rich tapestry of existence where gods, giants, and mortals all play their part.

Reflective Questions

- How do the interactions between the realms, such as the relationship between Asgard and Jotunheim, reflect the balance between order and chaos in Norse mythology?
- What role do the realms of Niflheim and Muspelheim play in the Norse understanding of creation and destruction, and how do they influence the prophecy of Ragnarok?
- How do the distinctions between realms like Valhalla, Fólkvangr, and Helheim illustrate the Norse view of the afterlife and the value placed on heroism, fate, and honor in death?

2.9 MYTHOLOGY QUIZ 2

Test your knowledge of the Nine Realms and their significance in Norse mythology with the following questions:

1. **Which realm is home to the Vanir gods, associated with fertility and prosperity?**

    A) Vanaheim

    B) Jotunheim

    C) Alfheim

    D) Asgard

2. **Who rules over Helheim, the realm of the dead?**

    A) Freyja

    B) Loki

    C) Odin

    D) Hel

3. **What two realms are considered the sources of elemental ice and fire in Norse cosmology?**

    A) Midgard and Alfheim

    B) Asgard and Vanaheim

    C) Niflheim and Muspelheim

    D) Helheim and Svartalfheim

4. **Which of the following is NOT a characteristic of Jotunheim?**

   A) It is the home of the giants.

   B) It is a realm associated with order and peace.

   C) It is often in conflict with Asgard.

   D) It is a realm of chaos and wilderness.

5. **What is the significance of the Gjallarbrú in Norse mythology?**

   A) It is the bridge that connects Asgard to Midgard.

   B) It is the river that surrounds Jotunheim.

   C) It is the bridge that souls cross to enter Helheim.

   D) It is the path leading to Valhalla.

6. **Which of these realms is home to the dwarves, known for their craftsmanship?**

   A) Muspelheim

   B) Alfheim

   C) Svartalfheim

   D) Jotunheim

Note: Answers to the quiz can be found in the "Answer Key" section in the Appendix.

CHAPTER 3:
THE MAJOR GODS OF ASGARD

3.1 ODIN: THE ALLFATHER

Odin, known as the **Allfather**, stands as one of the most important and complex figures in Norse mythology. As the king of the Aesir gods and the ruler of **Asgard**, Odin's influence stretches far beyond his realm. He is not just a god of power and leadership but also of **wisdom, sacrifice**, and the unrelenting pursuit of knowledge. His desire to understand the mysteries of the universe drives much of his mythological narrative, and his role in **Ragnarok**, the end of the world, underscores his deep connection to fate and destiny.

Odin's Quest for Wisdom

Unlike many gods in mythology who are born with great power or knowledge, Odin's journey is one of constant learning and sacrifice. He craves wisdom more than any other treasure, seeking out the secrets of the cosmos, especially those tied to **fate**. One of the most significant stories of Odin's quest for knowledge is his sacrifice at **Mimir's well**, a legendary well of wisdom that lay beneath one of the roots of **Yggdrasil**, the World Tree. In exchange for a drink from the well, Odin gave up one of his eyes, leaving him with a single, all-seeing eye that symbolizes his extraordinary vision and understanding of the world.

Odin's thirst for wisdom did not end there. In another myth, Odin sought to uncover the power of the **runes**, the magical symbols that govern fate and the forces of the cosmos. To unlock their secrets, he hung himself from a branch of Yggdrasil for nine days and nine nights, sacrificing himself to himself in a powerful ritual of suffering and revelation. During this time, Odin endured great pain, without food or water, until he finally glimpsed the runes and their meaning. This self-sacrifice allowed him to gain control over the runes, giving him knowledge of the forces that bind the universe.

Odin's relentless pursuit of wisdom reveals his belief that **knowledge and understanding** are the most potent forms of power. Unlike Thor, who wields physical strength to protect the realms, Odin's strength lies in his ability to see the threads of fate, prepare for the future, and make the hard decisions that others cannot.

Odin's Knowledge of Runes and Magic

The **runes**, which Odin discovered during his ritual of self-sacrifice, are more than mere symbols; they are believed to control the very fabric of reality. Each rune holds magical power, influencing aspects of life like fate, protection, and war. With the knowledge of these runes, Odin gained the ability to cast powerful spells, read the future, and even communicate with the dead. This connection to the runes also reflects Odin's association with **magic** in Norse mythology.

Odin is frequently depicted as a **sorcerer**, skilled in **Seidr**, a form of magic used to alter destiny. This magical ability made him feared and respected by both gods and mortals. His mastery over the runes and his magical prowess are often shown as tools he uses not only to maintain order in the cosmos but to gain an advantage over his enemies, including the giants who constantly threaten the stability of the world.

Odin's Role in Ragnarok

Odin's understanding of fate and destiny is intricately tied to his knowledge of **Ragnarok**, the prophesied end of the world. Unlike other gods who live in blissful ignorance of their fates, Odin knows all too well what the future holds. Through his wisdom and foresight, Odin understands that **Ragnarok** is inevitable, a cataclysmic battle that will bring about the destruction of the gods, including his own death. Yet, despite this knowledge, Odin does not shrink from his fate; instead, he prepares for it.

In the final battle of Ragnarok, Odin will face his greatest enemy, the monstrous wolf **Fenrir**, a beast born from the union of Loki and the giantess Angrboda. Fenrir, growing ever stronger, will eventually break free from the chains that bind him and devour Odin. Knowing this, Odin spends much of his time in preparation for the final battle. He gathers the bravest and most valiant warriors from **Midgard**, bringing them to **Valhalla**, his great hall of the fallen. There, they prepare for the inevitable day when they will fight alongside Odin against the forces of chaos.

Despite his efforts to delay the end, Odin understands that **fate cannot be changed**. His death at the hands of Fenrir represents the inevitability of chaos and destruction, even for the gods. However, Odin's acceptance of his fate is a testament to his wisdom—he knows that Ragnarok is not the end but a necessary cycle that will give birth to a new world. His role in Ragnarok, therefore, is not one of despair but of acceptance and preparation, demonstrating his unyielding strength and foresight.

Cultural Impact and Legacy

Odin's quest for wisdom, mastery of the runes, and foreknowledge of Ragnarok make him one of the most revered and feared gods in Norse mythology. He represents the duality of power and sacrifice, showing that even the mightiest of gods must endure pain and loss to achieve greatness. His willingness to sacrifice for knowledge reflects the Norse emphasis on the value of understanding and foresight over brute strength alone.

Odin's legacy extends beyond his mythological role into the cultural identity of the Norse people. As a **warrior god**, he embodies the values of courage and preparation for battle, and his **sacrifices** speak to the importance of enduring hardship in the pursuit of wisdom. For the Vikings, Odin was a symbol of the warrior ethos—one who not only fought with strength but with cunning and foresight. His acceptance of fate and death in Ragnarok also resonated deeply with the Norse, who believed that meeting one's end with honor was the highest form of glory.

Through Odin, the Norse people saw the complexity of leadership, the weight of responsibility, and the importance of knowledge in navigating the often harsh and chaotic world in which they lived. His myths continue to inspire those who seek wisdom, even in the face of inevitable challenges and difficult truths.

3.2 THOR: THE THUNDER GOD

In Norse mythology, **Thor**, the **God of Thunder**, stands as the protector of **Midgard**, the realm of humans, and one of the most beloved and powerful figures in the entire pantheon. Unlike his father, Odin, who seeks wisdom and uses magic, Thor's strength lies in his **brute force**, his courage, and his unyielding will to protect both gods and mortals from the forces of chaos. Wielding his mighty hammer, **Mjolnir**, Thor is the Aesir's greatest warrior, and his battles, particularly against the giants (Jotun), define his role as a guardian and enforcer of cosmic order.

Thor's Protection of Midgard

Thor's primary duty is to safeguard Midgard, the world of humans, from the many threats that arise from the other realms. As the protector of humanity, Thor is deeply connected to the everyday life of the Norse people. Farmers, warriors, and common folk alike would often call upon Thor's strength in prayers for protection against storms, enemies, and other dangers. He was a **god of the people**, known for his approachable nature, immense strength, and dedication to maintaining the order of the cosmos.

Thor's home is in **Asgard**, but his heart belongs to Midgard. His responsibility as a protector is most famously symbolized by his **hammer, Mjolnir**, a weapon of unparalleled power. With Mjolnir, Thor is able to summon thunder and lightning, smash through mountains, and obliterate his enemies. More importantly, Mjolnir is also a tool of **blessing**. It is said that Thor used his hammer to consecrate marriages, bless crops, and even bring the dead back to life, further highlighting his role as a guardian of both physical and spiritual well-being.

Thor's unbreakable bond with Midgard is most evident in his constant battle with the **giants**, who represent the forces of chaos that threaten the realms. As the natural enemies of the gods, the giants are always seeking to undermine the order that Thor and the Aesir work so hard to protect. Whether battling giants in the mountains of Jotunheim or standing guard over Midgard, Thor's tireless fight against these enemies is central to his identity.

Thor's Battles Against the Giants

The most defining aspect of Thor's mythology is his endless war with the **Jotun** (giants), who are often depicted as monstrous beings that seek to bring chaos and destruction to the Nine Realms. The giants embody the unpredictable and wild forces of nature—storms, earthquakes, and the harsh landscapes that the Norse people faced in their daily lives. Thor's role as their protector places him in constant conflict with these primal forces, and his battles are legendary.

One of Thor's most famous encounters with the giants is his battle with the **giant Hrungnir**. Hrungnir, a stone-hearted giant, boasted that he was stronger than any of the gods. Thor, naturally, accepted the challenge and faced Hrungnir in a duel. In a fierce battle, Thor struck Hrungnir with Mjolnir, crushing the giant and proving once again that the forces of chaos could not overcome the power of Asgard's champion.

Another well-known tale recounts Thor's journey to **Utgard**, the land of the giants, where he competed in a series of challenges set by the giant king, **Utgarda-Loki**. These contests, meant to humiliate Thor, tested his strength and endurance. Though the giants used illusions to deceive him, Thor's sheer might and determination impressed even his enemies, demonstrating his unwavering resolve to protect the cosmos from their trickery and power.

One of the most significant battles in Thor's mythological arc is his prophesied fight with **Jormungandr**, the **World Serpent**, during **Ragnarok**. Jormungandr is one of the greatest enemies of the gods, a monstrous serpent so large that it encircles the entirety of Midgard. The rivalry between Thor and Jormungandr is one of the central conflicts leading up to Ragnarok. It is foretold that in the final battle, Thor will finally slay the World Serpent, but not before being poisoned by its venom, leading to his own death shortly after his victory. This fated confrontation marks Thor as a hero willing to sacrifice his life for the protection of the world, reinforcing the idea that even the gods are not immune to fate.

Thor as a Symbol of Strength and Order

While Thor is often seen as a warrior, he is also a symbol of **order** in Norse mythology. His constant battles against the giants are more than physical fights—they represent the ongoing struggle between **order and chaos**, a key theme in the Norse worldview.

The giants, as forces of nature, challenge the structure of the universe, while Thor, as the enforcer of order, works tirelessly to keep them at bay.

In addition to his physical prowess, Thor is also characterized by his **stubbornness** and sometimes **hot-headed nature**. He is quick to anger and faster to act, often rushing into situations with his hammer before thinking things through. This makes him a somewhat flawed but deeply relatable figure in Norse mythology. His faults are seen not as weaknesses but as reminders that even the mightiest of gods have their imperfections, and that true strength comes from perseverance and unwavering dedication to a cause.

Cultural Impact and Legacy

Thor's impact on Norse culture is immense. He was one of the most widely worshipped gods, especially among the common people, who saw in him a protector of their homes, families, and livelihoods. His hammer, Mjolnir, became a symbol of **protection**, and miniature versions of Mjolnir were worn as amulets for good luck and safety. In Viking culture, Thor was the embodiment of courage, strength, and loyalty—values that were deeply cherished by the Norse people.

Thor's legacy extends far beyond ancient mythology. In modern times, he remains a cultural icon, appearing in literature, art, and even popular media. The image of Thor, with his powerful hammer and lightning-filled skies, continues to captivate the imagination. His figure has been adapted in everything from **comic books** and **movies** to modern **fantasy literature**, where he is often portrayed as the archetypal hero—strong, brave, and willing to sacrifice everything to protect those he loves.

For the ancient Norse, Thor was more than just a god of strength—he was the **protector** of their world and their way of life. His unending battle against the forces of chaos resonated deeply with a people who lived in a harsh, unpredictable environment. The enduring popularity of Thor reflects not just admiration for his physical power, but also a deep respect for his role as a guardian of order and his willingness to confront the darker, more dangerous forces of existence.

Thor's impact on modern culture can also be seen in the continued use of **Mjolnir** as a symbol of protection and strength, not only in religious or cultural contexts but also as a symbol of personal empowerment. His influence stretches from the Viking Age to contemporary depictions, making him one of the most enduring and beloved figures in Norse mythology.

3.3 LOKI: THE TRICKSTER GOD

Few figures in Norse mythology are as complex and contradictory as **Loki**, the **Trickster God**. Unlike Odin, who seeks wisdom, or Thor, who protects Midgard, Loki is driven by a far more unpredictable and chaotic nature. He is a god of **mischief**, **deception**, and **transformation**, and his actions have profound consequences for both gods and mortals. However, Loki's role cannot be easily defined as purely good or evil. He is both a **helper** and a **villain**, a force of ingenuity and destruction, making him one of the most fascinating characters in Norse mythology.

Loki as a Helper and Ally of the Gods

Loki is often seen as an ally to the gods, particularly in the early myths, where his cunning and quick thinking help the gods out of difficult situations. His shape-shifting abilities allow him to transform into any creature, helping him solve problems or create mischief that often ends in unexpected benefits. In many ways, Loki serves as a **mediator** between the gods and the giants, as he himself is of **Jotun** origin, born of giants but accepted into the company of the Aesir.

One of Loki's most famous acts of cunning involves his role in securing the great treasures of the gods, including **Mjolnir**, Thor's mighty hammer. In this tale, Loki is responsible for losing **Sif's golden hair** (Thor's wife) and must make amends by seeking out the skilled dwarves to craft new hair for her. In the process, Loki's deceit leads to the creation of Mjolnir, **Odin's spear Gungnir**, and **Freyr's golden boar**, all key artifacts in Norse mythology. Although his mischief initially causes trouble, his actions ultimately benefit the gods, reflecting his unpredictable but helpful nature.

Another instance where Loki assists the gods is when he helps Thor recover Mjolnir after it is stolen by the giant **Thrym**, who demands Freyja's hand in marriage in exchange for the hammer. Loki devises a plan for Thor to disguise himself as Freyja, fooling Thrym and retrieving the hammer, once again using his cunning to aid the gods in their struggle against the giants.

Loki as a Villain and Agent of Chaos

As much as Loki helps the gods, he is equally known for his role in bringing chaos and tragedy to Asgard. His trickster nature means that he thrives on **disruption**, and his actions often lead to devastating consequences. Over time, Loki's mischief turns darker, and he increasingly becomes an **agent of destruction**.

Loki's most infamous act is his involvement in the death of **Baldur**, the beloved son of Odin and Frigg. Baldur's death is a pivotal event in Norse mythology, signaling the beginning of the end, or **Ragnarok**. After learning that Baldur is immune to all forms of harm, except for mistletoe, Loki fashions an arrow out of the plant and tricks Baldur's blind brother, **Hodr**, into unknowingly killing him. This act of cruelty leads to immense grief among the gods, particularly for Odin and Frigg, and sets the stage for Ragnarok, the prophesied destruction of the gods.

Loki's villainy does not end with Baldur's death. After his actions are uncovered, he is punished and **imprisoned** by the gods. He is bound to a rock, where a serpent drips venom onto his face, causing him great pain. His wife, **Sigyn**, remains by his side, catching the venom in a bowl to ease his suffering, but every time she empties the bowl, the venom causes Loki to writhe in agony, creating earthquakes in Midgard.

Loki's Role in Ragnarok

Loki's role as a **villain** reaches its peak during **Ragnarok**, the final battle that will bring about the end of the gods. It is foretold that Loki will break free from his bonds and join the forces of chaos, leading the giants and monstrous creatures in their assault on Asgard. He will sail the ship **Naglfar**, made from the fingernails of the dead, and stand alongside his monstrous children—**Fenrir**, the wolf who devours Odin, and **Jormungandr**, the World Serpent that will battle Thor.

During Ragnarok, Loki himself will face **Heimdall**, the watchman of the gods, in a fateful duel. Both will perish, marking the end of their rivalry and further solidifying Loki's place as a bringer of destruction. However, even in this ultimate act of betrayal, Loki's role is essential to the cosmic cycle of creation and destruction that defines Norse mythology. His actions, while devastating, are part of the inevitable **fate** that drives the universe toward rebirth after Ragnarok.

Symbolism and Cultural Impact

Loki's complex nature as both a **helper** and a **villain** symbolizes the duality of **chaos and order** in Norse mythology. He is a god who cannot be categorized easily, reflecting the unpredictability of life itself. In Loki, the Norse found a character who embodied both the **creative** and **destructive** aspects of chaos. He is a reminder that even in a world governed by fate, disruption and change are necessary parts of the cosmic balance.

In many ways, Loki's role reflects the darker side of Norse society, where cunning and deceit were sometimes necessary for survival in a harsh, unforgiving environment. His actions, while often causing harm, also serve as **catalysts** for change, showing that chaos is not inherently evil but a force that brings transformation.

In modern times, Loki has remained a popular and intriguing figure, appearing in literature, art, and contemporary media, often portrayed as an anti-hero rather than a straightforward villain. His character continues to captivate audiences with his complexity, his ability to straddle the line between good and evil, and his role as the ultimate trickster in a world where nothing is ever certain.

Loki's legacy as a **shapeshifter**, a **deceiver**, and a **betrayer** leaves a lasting impression on Norse mythology. He represents the unpredictability of fate and the inevitability of change, making him an essential figure in the cosmic balance between the forces of order and chaos.

3.4 FREYJA: THE GODDESS OF LOVE AND WAR

Among the most powerful and revered deities in Norse mythology, **Freyja** stands out not only for her beauty but also for her complex and multifaceted nature. As the **Goddess of Love**, **Fertility**, and **War**, Freyja embodies a unique combination of tenderness and strength. While she is often associated with matters of the heart—love, desire, and fertility—she also plays a critical role in the brutal realities of war, leading fallen warriors to her own hall, **Folkvangr**. This duality makes Freyja one of the most fascinating figures in the Norse pantheon, capable of bringing both life and death in equal measure.

Freyja's Role in Love and Fertility

Freyja's connection to **love** and **fertility** is perhaps her most well-known aspect. As a goddess of love and desire, Freyja oversees the union of couples, the flourishing of crops, and the creation of life. Her presence was invoked during weddings, harvests, and times of birth, symbolizing the life-giving powers that were central to the survival and prosperity of the Norse people. As the goddess of **fertility**, she also governs the earth's cycles, ensuring that the land remains fertile and that new life is constantly brought into the world.

Freyja is often depicted as a goddess of **irresistible beauty**, adorned with jewelry, including her most prized possession, the **Brísingamen necklace**, a symbol of her allure and power. According to legend, Freyja obtained the Brísingamen after making a deal with four dwarves, who crafted the necklace in exchange for a night with her. This tale underscores her deep association with desire and sensuality, but it also highlights her autonomy and willingness to make decisions in pursuit of what she values most.

Despite her associations with love and beauty, Freyja is far from a passive figure. Her desire for **freedom** and **independence** sets her apart from other goddesses. She is not bound by conventional expectations and instead navigates the world of gods and mortals with grace, wit, and determination. Freyja's strength lies in her ability to balance the softness of love with the harsh realities of life, making her a goddess who is both relatable and deeply revered.

Freyja's Role in Battle and War

Though she is often associated with love, Freyja's **warrior aspect** is just as prominent. Freyja is not only a goddess of creation but also of **death** and **destruction**—a duality that reflects the Norse understanding of life's cycles. In Norse mythology, Freyja chooses half of the slain warriors from the battlefield to reside in her hall, **Folkvangr** ("Field of the People"). The other half are taken to

Valhalla, Odin's hall. This role makes Freyja a powerful figure in the aftermath of battle, deciding the fates of warriors and preparing them for the afterlife.

Her connection to battle is closely tied to her mastery of **Seidr**, a form of Norse magic that allows practitioners to alter fate, communicate with the dead, and predict the future. Freyja is considered the most skilled Seidr practitioner among the gods, and she is often invoked for her ability to influence outcomes in both love and war. Her magical prowess, combined with her warrior spirit, makes her a formidable force in Norse mythology, one who embodies both the creation of life and the inevitable destruction that comes with war.

Freyja's role in battle goes beyond merely selecting the dead. As a goddess of war, she represents the **fierceness** and **bravery** required of both men and women in Norse society. She is frequently seen riding into battle on her **chariot**, pulled by two large cats, a symbol of her strength and independence. Her courage in the face of war, coupled with her deep connection to love and life, underscores the Norse belief that death and rebirth are intrinsically linked.

Freyja's Dual Nature: Love and War

Freyja's duality is perhaps her most defining trait. As the goddess of both love and war, she embodies the tension between creation and destruction, beauty and brutality. In many ways, Freyja represents the full spectrum of human experience, from the tenderness of love to the harshness of conflict. This balance between seemingly opposing forces is a recurring theme in Norse mythology, where gods and goddesses often play multiple roles and embrace complexity in their characters.

In love, Freyja is seen as a **protector of the heart**, guiding individuals toward passion, desire, and emotional fulfillment. She governs the forces of attraction, romance, and fertility, ensuring that life continues to flourish. But in war, Freyja is equally powerful, leading warriors into battle, overseeing their fate, and ensuring that those who die in combat are honored in the afterlife. Her role in both realms shows her capacity for deep emotion and her strength as a leader, making her an essential figure in Norse culture.

Symbolism and Cultural Impact

Freyja's influence reaches far beyond the battlefield and the hearth. She is a symbol of **femininity, independence**, and the **duality of life**. For the Norse people, Freyja represented the powerful women in their society who could be both nurturing and fierce. Her mastery of Seidr and her connection to both life and death reflect the deep respect the Norse had for women's roles in both domestic and warlike contexts.

Freyja's legacy continues to resonate today, as she remains a symbol of strength and empowerment. Her ability to move seamlessly between the worlds of love and war speaks to the complexity of human nature and the idea that true power lies in embracing all aspects of oneself. In modern depictions, Freyja is often portrayed as a fierce warrior goddess, but her role as a goddess of love and fertility is equally emphasized, making her one of the most well-rounded deities in Norse mythology.

Through her stories, Freyja teaches that life is a balance of opposites—love and conflict, beauty and strength—and that both are necessary to maintain the harmony of the universe. Her cultural impact is felt not only in the way the Norse viewed women and warfare but also in how they understood the cycles of life, death, and rebirth.

In Norse mythology, **Heimdall** holds the crucial role of **Guardian of the Bifrost**, the shimmering **rainbow bridge** that connects **Midgard** (the realm of humans) to **Asgard** (the realm of the gods). As the ever-vigilant watchman of the gods, Heimdall's task is to protect Asgard from any threats, especially those posed by the giants (Jotun), and to sound the alarm when danger approaches. His extraordinary senses and unwavering vigilance make him a key figure in the protection of the gods, but his role extends beyond mere guardianship. Heimdall plays an essential part in the Norse apocalypse, **Ragnarok**, where his fate is tied to the final confrontation between order and chaos.

Heimdall's Eternal Vigilance

Heimdall's primary duty is to guard the **Bifrost**, the rainbow bridge that serves as the only passage between the mortal world and Asgard. His station at the bridge marks him as the first line of defense for the gods, watching for any who would dare threaten their realm. Heimdall's senses are legendary—he is said to have such keen **eyesight** that he can see for hundreds of miles, even in complete darkness. His **hearing** is equally impressive; he can hear grass growing and the wool growing on sheep, making it nearly impossible for anyone to approach Asgard without his knowledge.

In addition to his heightened senses, Heimdall is known for his **endurance**. He does not require sleep, allowing him to maintain his eternal watch over the realms. His vigilance is unyielding, as he knows that the greatest threat to the gods—**Ragnarok**—is inevitable. Heimdall's duty is to ensure that the gods are prepared for this final battle and to protect the balance of the cosmos for as long as possible.

Heimdall is often depicted standing at the entrance to the Bifrost, fully armored and ready to defend the bridge with his sword. He carries the **Gjallarhorn**, a great horn whose sound can be heard across all the worlds. It is this horn that will announce the beginning of Ragnarok, signaling the start of the end for the gods and the universe as they know it.

Heimdall's Role in the Apocalypse

Heimdall's watchfulness is most critical in the events leading up to **Ragnarok**, the prophesied end of the world. As the harbinger of this great battle, Heimdall's task is to sound the Gjallarhorn when the forces of chaos—led by **Loki** and the giants—begin their assault on Asgard. When the Gjallarhorn is blown, it will echo across the

Nine Realms, alerting the gods that Ragnarok has begun and that the final conflict is at hand.

In the battle of Ragnarok, Heimdall faces his greatest challenge as he confronts **Loki**, the trickster god who will lead the forces of chaos against the Aesir. The two are sworn enemies, with Heimdall representing **order** and **vigilance**, while Loki embodies **chaos** and **deceit**. The enmity between them is deeply rooted in Norse mythology, culminating in their fateful confrontation during the apocalypse.

It is foretold that Heimdall and Loki will meet in a final, deadly duel during **Ragnarok**. In this climactic battle, both Heimdall and Loki will strike each other down, leading to their mutual destruction. Heimdall's death marks the ultimate sacrifice of the guardian who has spent eons protecting Asgard from the forces of chaos. His willingness to face Loki, despite knowing the outcome, underscores his unwavering commitment to his duty and the protection of the realms.

Even though Heimdall's fate is sealed in Ragnarok, his role in the apocalypse is essential to the cosmic cycle of creation, destruction, and rebirth that defines Norse mythology. His death, like that of many other gods, is not seen as a failure but rather a necessary part of the inevitable cycle that will lead to the rebirth of the world. Heimdall's sacrifice in Ragnarok is symbolic of the **eternal struggle between order and chaos**, where the forces of stability can hold off destruction for only so long, but ultimately, the world must be renewed through conflict.

Symbolism and Cultural Impact

Heimdall's role as the **eternal watchman** and guardian of the Bifrost represents the vigilance and readiness necessary to protect the fragile balance of the cosmos. His sharp senses and tireless watchfulness reflect the Norse belief that danger is always looming, and that constant vigilance is required to preserve order in a world filled with chaos.

In Norse culture, Heimdall's character also symbolizes the value of **sacrifice** for the greater good. His destiny is to die in battle against Loki, but he embraces this fate with honor, knowing that his sacrifice will protect Asgard and the cosmos for as long as possible. Heimdall's role in mythology serves as a reminder that the forces of chaos can never be fully eradicated, but they can be delayed through courage and dedication.

Heimdall continues to have a lasting impact on modern depictions of Norse mythology, often portrayed as the ultimate guardian and symbol of loyalty. His character resonates with themes of duty, protection, and the inevitable clash between order and chaos that defines much of Norse cosmology.

3.6 SUMMARY AND KEY TAKEAWAYS

Summary

In this chapter, we explored some of the major gods of Asgard, each playing a unique role in the defense, leadership, and balance of the cosmos. These deities are central to the Norse understanding of fate, honor, and the eternal struggle between order and chaos, shaping not only the world of the gods but also the lives of mortals.

Odin: The Allfather

Odin is the king of the Aesir gods, known for his relentless quest for wisdom. Through personal sacrifice, including the loss of his eye and hanging from Yggdrasil for nine days, Odin gains knowledge of the **runes** and the secrets of fate. His wisdom allows him to foresee the events of **Ragnarok**, and his leadership prepares Asgard for this inevitable end, where he will meet his fate in battle against **Fenrir**.

Thor: The Thunder God

Thor, the God of Thunder, serves as the protector of **Midgard** and Asgard, using his mighty hammer **Mjolnir** to defend against the giants (Jotun), who represent the forces of chaos. His strength and courage are unmatched, and his tireless battles against the giants, especially his prophesied clash with **Jormungandr** during Ragnarok, make him a symbol of unyielding defense and the fight to maintain cosmic order.

Loki: The Trickster God

Loki, the Trickster, embodies both mischief and betrayal. His role is often ambiguous as he alternates between aiding the gods with his cunning and bringing chaos through his deceptions. His most infamous act is the murder of **Baldur**, which sets the stage for Ragnarok. Ultimately, Loki will turn against the gods during the final battle, aligning himself with the giants and leading the forces of chaos.

Freyja: The Goddess of Love and War

Freyja, the goddess of love, fertility, and war, represents the duality of creation and destruction. As a goddess of fertility, she is invoked for prosperity and abundance. However, she also leads fallen warriors to her hall, **Folkvangr**, making her a key figure in war and death. Her mastery of **Seidr** (Norse magic) allows her to manipulate fate and destiny, further highlighting her complex nature as both a nurturer and a warrior.

Heimdall: The Guardian of the Bifrost

Heimdall is the ever-vigilant guardian of the **Bifrost**, the rainbow bridge connecting Midgard to Asgard. With his extraordinary senses and the Gjallarhorn, Heimdall stands watch over Asgard, awaiting the moment he will sound the alarm for **Ragnarok**. In the final battle, he will face his rival, **Loki**, resulting in their mutual destruction, marking Heimdall's role as both protector and a harbinger of the apocalypse.

Key Takeaways:

1. **Odin's Quest for Knowledge**: Odin's unquenchable thirst for wisdom through sacrifice, especially through his knowledge of the runes and his foresight into Ragnarok, demonstrates his role as both a leader and a seeker of hidden truths.

2. **Thor's Protection of Order**: Thor's battles against the giants represent the Norse belief in the struggle between order and chaos. His strength and courage make him the ultimate protector of Midgard and a symbol of unrelenting force against destruction.

3. **Loki's Dual Nature**: Loki's role as both a helper and villain emphasizes the complexity of his character. His shift from aiding the gods to bringing about their downfall in Ragnarok reflects the unpredictability and duality of chaos.

4. **Freyja's Balance of Love and War**: Freyja's duality as a goddess of both fertility and battle illustrates the Norse view of life's cycles, where love and war, creation and destruction, are deeply intertwined and equally necessary.

5. **Heimdall's Vigilance and Sacrifice**: Heimdall's eternal watch over the Bifrost and his foretold confrontation with Loki during Ragnarok symbolize the importance of vigilance, sacrifice, and readiness in the face of inevitable destruction and renewal.

These gods represent the core values and struggles of Norse mythology, where balance, fate, and the cyclical nature of life and death dominate their stories and influence the world of gods and mortals.

Reflective Questions

- How does Odin's pursuit of wisdom and knowledge through personal sacrifice reflect the Norse values of leadership and preparation for inevitable fate, particularly in relation to Ragnarok?
- In what ways do Thor's battles against the giants symbolize the ongoing struggle between order and chaos? How does his role as protector of Midgard resonate with the everyday challenges faced by the Norse people?
- Loki's dual nature as both a helper and a betrayer presents him as a complex figure in Norse mythology. How does his character challenge traditional notions of good and evil, and what might his actions reveal about the balance of creation and destruction in the Norse cosmos?

3.7 MYTHOLOGY QUIZ 3

Test your knowledge about the Olympian gods with the following questions:

1. **What did Odin sacrifice in exchange for wisdom from Mimir's well?**

    A) His hammer

    B) His eye

    C) His spear

    D) His life

2. **What is the name of Thor's mighty hammer?**

    A) Gungnir

    B) Brísingamen

    C) Mjolnir

    D) Gjallarhorn

3. **Who is prophesied to kill Odin during Ragnarok?**

    A) Loki

    B) Jormungandr

    C) Fenrir

    D) Surtr

4. **Freyja leads half of the fallen warriors to which hall after battle?**

    A) Valhalla

    B) Folkvangr

    C) Helheim

    D) Vanaheim

5. **What weapon does Heimdall use to signal the beginning of Ragnarok?**

    A) Gjallarhorn

    B) Mjolnir

    C) Gungnir

    D) Skidbladnir

6. **Which god is both a helper and a villain in Norse mythology, responsible for the death of Baldur?**

    A) Thor

    B) Loki

    C) Odin

    D) Tyr

7. **What is the name of the rainbow bridge that Heimdall guards?**

A) Yggdrasil

B) Gjallarhorn

C) Bifrost

D) Utgard

Note: Answers to the quiz can be found in the "Answer Key" section in the Appendix.

CHAPTER 4:
HEROES AND MORTALS

In Norse culture, the **sagas** are an essential form of storytelling, weaving together elements of **mythology, history, and heroic deeds** into epic narratives that have endured for centuries. These sagas not only recount the adventures of legendary heroes but also preserve the cultural values, struggles, and beliefs of the Norse people. They are a unique blend of historical events and mythological motifs, making them a vital part of the way the Norse viewed their world—one where gods and mortals coexisted and where human bravery could rival even the mightiest of divine acts.

What are the Sagas?

The **sagas** are long, narrative prose works that tell the stories of **heroes, kings, and families**. Often set in the Viking Age, they reflect the harsh realities of life in medieval Scandinavia, including **family feuds, territorial conquests**, and **explorations** of distant lands. While the sagas contain elements of historical fact, such as the lives of real kings and warriors, they also intertwine these facts with mythological elements, creating a bridge between the **historical and the fantastical**.

One of the most defining aspects of the sagas is their focus on **heroic characters** who display traits highly valued by the Norse: **bravery, honor, loyalty, and wisdom**. These sagas often depict how the heroes' deeds affect both the mortal and divine realms, showing that the destinies of men were deeply entwined with the will of the gods. Unlike in many modern myths, the heroes of these sagas are not always victorious or morally perfect—they often face tragic outcomes, reflecting the Norse belief in the inevitability of fate.

Sagas and the Blurring of Mythology and History

The sagas are a powerful blend of **mythology and history**, making it difficult to separate historical fact from legend. Some sagas feature legendary heroes whose deeds seem to transcend human ability, pushing them into the realm of myth. However, the same sagas may also include references to actual historical events or locations, grounding these mythical figures in reality. This fusion reflects the Norse worldview, where gods, spirits, and supernatural forces were deeply embedded in everyday life.

For example, the **Saga of the Volsungs**—one of the most famous sagas—blends mythology with the exploits of the heroic **Sigurd**, the dragon-slayer. While the saga recounts Sigurd's legendary battle with the dragon **Fafnir**, it also deals with themes such as family loyalty, betrayal, and the inevitability of fate, reflecting the real-life struggles of the Norse people. Similarly, other sagas often include gods like **Odin** or **Thor**, who interact with mortals, guiding or testing them, and bringing their influence to the world of men.

These stories served not only as entertainment but also as **moral guides** and **cultural touchstones**, helping to define what it meant to be a hero in Norse society. Through their larger-than-life deeds, these heroes demonstrated the values that were important to the Norse people: **strength in battle, loyalty to family and kin, and a steadfast acceptance of fate**.

The Importance of Sagas in Norse Culture

Sagas were passed down orally for generations before being written down in later centuries, primarily during the **13th century**, after Christianity had already spread to the region. Despite this, they remain some of the most significant sources of knowledge about **Viking Age society** and Norse beliefs. The sagas preserved in texts like the **Poetic Edda** and the **Prose Edda** provide insight into how the Norse viewed their world, their relationship with the gods, and the qualities they admired in both gods and men.

One of the most significant features of the sagas is their emphasis on **fate**—a central concept in Norse culture. The heroes of these stories often fight against insurmountable odds, fully aware that their fates are predetermined by the **Norns** (the Norse goddesses of destiny), but they do so with **courage and honor**. The sagas show that even in the face of certain death or failure, it was the **struggle itself** that defined a hero.

These narratives also reflect the **political and social realities** of the time. Many sagas focus on themes of **family loyalty, vengeance, and feuds**, mirroring the legal and social structures of the Norse world, where blood ties and oaths were of the utmost importance. Heroes often sought revenge for wrongs done to their families, and the resolution of these conflicts—sometimes through violence, sometimes through diplomacy—was a recurring theme.

Cultural Impact and Legacy

The sagas have had a profound impact on how Norse culture has been remembered and interpreted throughout history. Not only do they offer a window into the Viking Age, but they also reveal the **timeless themes** of heroism, fate, and the human condition. Their blending of history with myth created a unique narrative form that has influenced modern literature, films, and storytelling.

The sagas' enduring appeal lies in their ability to capture the **epic struggles** of individuals against the forces of nature, society, and destiny. Through their tales of kings, warriors, and legendary beasts, the sagas have continued to inspire new generations, keeping the spirit of Norse culture alive in modern storytelling.

4.2 SIGURD AND THE DRAGON FAFNIR

One of the most famous tales in Norse mythology is the **epic saga of Sigurd**, the legendary hero who slayed the dragon **Fafnir**. This story, which blends themes of bravery, betrayal, and cursed wealth, stands as one of the greatest heroic narratives in the entire Norse tradition. Sigurd's triumph over Fafnir and his acquisition of the cursed treasure form the heart of this tale, offering a vivid portrayal of the complexities of fate, greed, and heroism.

The Dragon Fafnir and the Cursed Treasure

Fafnir was once a dwarf, the son of **Hreidmar**, who came into possession of a massive treasure, originally taken from the god **Loki** as compensation for the death of Hreidmar's son. This hoard of gold, however, was cursed by the god of mischief, and its greed-inducing power corrupted Fafnir. Overcome by greed, Fafnir killed his own father to claim the treasure for himself. In a twisted act of self-preservation and paranoia, Fafnir transformed into a **dragon**, guarding his hoard in isolation, driven mad by the curse that consumed him.

The image of Fafnir as a dragon is emblematic of the mythological link between **greed and monstrosity**. He is no longer the dwarf he once was but a monstrous embodiment of greed itself, hoarding the cursed treasure that would ultimately lead to his downfall. Fafnir's treasure, though immense, is tainted by Loki's curse, ensuring that anyone who seeks it will meet a tragic end.

Sigurd's Quest

The hero **Sigurd** (or **Siegfried** in Germanic tradition) is a central figure in the **Volsunga Saga**, and his quest to slay Fafnir is driven by a combination of destiny, honor, and manipulation. Sigurd is tutored by the wise and cunning **Regin**, who happens to be Fafnir's brother. Regin, eager to reclaim the treasure from his dragon-turned-brother, urges Sigurd to undertake the dangerous task of killing Fafnir and retrieving the hoard. However, Regin's motivations are far from noble, as he seeks the treasure for himself.

Sigurd, though young, is a hero destined for greatness. Armed with the powerful sword **Gram**, reforged from the broken shards of his father's blade, Sigurd is a symbol of courage, strength, and the unbreakable ties of fate. Regin leads him to the lair of Fafnir, where Sigurd prepares to face the dragon. In a show of cleverness, Sigurd digs a trench and waits for Fafnir to crawl over it, allowing him to strike the beast from below and avoid the dragon's deadly breath.

When Fafnir approaches, Sigurd delivers a **fatal blow** to the dragon's belly, slaying the beast and securing his place among the greatest of Norse heroes. However, the tale of Sigurd does not end with his triumph over Fafnir; it is here that the **curse of the treasure** begins to take hold.

The Cursed Treasure and Its Consequences

As Fafnir lies dying, he warns Sigurd of the curse that hangs over the treasure, cautioning him about the inevitable tragedy that will follow anyone who claims it. Despite this, Sigurd takes the treasure, including the cursed **ring Andvaranaut**, which was originally enchanted by the dwarf Andvari under Loki's influence. This ring, like all the treasure it is part of, carries with it a dark fate.

After slaying Fafnir, Sigurd tastes the blood of the dragon, and in doing so, gains the ability to **understand the language of birds**. The birds warn Sigurd of Regin's treachery, revealing that Regin plans to kill him and take the treasure for himself. Acting on this new knowledge, Sigurd kills Regin before he can betray him, but in doing so, Sigurd becomes fully entangled in the curse of the treasure.

Though Sigurd now possesses Fafnir's treasure, it brings him no peace. He travels far, winning the love of the valkyrie **Brynhildr**, and for a time seems destined for happiness. However, the cursed gold and the ring eventually lead to betrayal and tragedy, as greed, jealousy, and fate conspire to destroy Sigurd's life. He is betrayed by those he trusts, and his death comes not in battle but through the **deceit** of others, a tragic reminder of the inescapable power of the curse.

Symbolism and Cultural Impact

The story of **Sigurd and Fafnir** is one of the greatest examples of the **heroic sagas** that blend mythology and history, offering a rich exploration of Norse cultural values. Sigurd's bravery and strength are the hallmarks of a true hero, yet his story is also a cautionary tale about the dangers of **greed** and the **inevitability of fate**. Even as Sigurd achieves the impossible by slaying the dragon, he cannot escape the curse that comes with the treasure.

Fafnir's transformation into a dragon symbolizes the destructive nature of greed, where the pursuit of wealth can turn even the noblest of beings into monsters. Sigurd's triumph, though impressive, is ultimately overshadowed by the tragic consequences of his actions, reflecting the Norse belief that **fate** is inescapable, no matter how heroic one may be.

The legacy of Sigurd's story extends far beyond Norse mythology. His tale has been retold in various forms throughout **Germanic** and **Scandinavian** literature, most notably in the **Nibelungenlied** and **Wagner's Ring Cycle**. His saga, like many of the Norse heroic narratives, continues to inspire modern interpretations in literature, film, and art, keeping the legend of Sigurd and Fafnir alive for new generations.

Cultural Impact and Legacy

The story of Sigurd slaying Fafnir serves as a powerful **moral lesson** about the dangers of unchecked ambition and the allure of cursed wealth. While Sigurd is celebrated for his bravery, his fate reflects the Norse understanding that even the greatest heroes are not immune to the **forces of fate**. The cursed treasure is a symbol of the **inevitable tragedy** that follows greed, reminding the Norse people that wealth, especially when acquired through deceit or violence, carries its own burden.

Sigurd's saga has endured for centuries, not just as a tale of dragon-slaying heroism but as a deeply **tragic story** that captures the complexities of Norse culture and the relentless power of fate.

Few figures in Norse history and legend stand as tall as **Ragnar Lodbrok**, the infamous **Viking king, warrior, and explorer** whose life has been immortalized in sagas and historical chronicles. His story is a blend of **myth and history**, with his legendary exploits stretching across Europe, where he became both feared and admired for his daring conquests. Ragnar's legacy is not only tied to his own achievements but also to his children, many of whom became famous in their own right. Perhaps most dramatically, Ragnar's death in a **snake pit** stands as one of the most iconic endings in Norse legend, symbolizing his indomitable spirit and unyielding defiance in the face of death.

Ragnar's Famous Conquests

Ragnar Lodbrok's legend begins with his reputation as a **fearless Viking raider** and **king**, whose exploits took him to distant lands, often leading daring attacks on coastal towns and cities throughout **England, France**, and beyond. His early raids on **Northumbria**, **Mercia**, and **Wessex** made Ragnar a name of terror among the Anglo-Saxons, where he and his warriors pillaged monasteries, seized land, and captured treasures. Ragnar's fleet, composed of longships filled with fierce warriors, was a force that devastated much of **Anglo-Saxon England** in the early Viking Age.

One of Ragnar's most famous and ambitious raids was his **siege of Paris** in **845 CE**. According to the sagas and historical accounts, Ragnar led a fleet of **120 ships** up the River Seine, attacking the city of Paris, then under the control of the Frankish king, **Charles the Bald**. The siege was a masterful display of Viking strategy and ruthlessness. Unable to defend the city, the Franks ultimately paid Ragnar a massive ransom—**7,000 pounds of silver**—to spare Paris from further destruction. This victory not only enriched Ragnar but also cemented his place as one of the most formidable Viking leaders of his time.

Ragnar's exploits extended far beyond France and England. Some sagas recount his adventures as far as the Mediterranean, where he was said to have raided along the coasts of **Spain** and **Italy**, a testament to his ambitions and the far-reaching influence of Viking raiders during the 9th century. Whether through myth or history, Ragnar's reputation as a **warrior-king** was built on his audacity and his ability to inspire loyalty among his men, many of whom became legendary figures themselves.

Ragnar's Death in the Snake Pit

While Ragnar's life was filled with daring conquests, it is his **death** that remains one of the most famous elements of his legend. According to the sagas, Ragnar's final campaign was in **Northumbria**, where he attempted to capture more lands. However, this raid did not go as planned. He was eventually captured by **King Ælla** of Northumbria, a rival who had long sought vengeance against Ragnar for his earlier attacks.

Upon his capture, King Ælla ordered Ragnar to be **executed** in a particularly brutal manner. The sagas recount that Ragnar was thrown into a **snake pit**, where he faced a slow and agonizing death. Yet, even in the face of certain doom, Ragnar remained defiant. According to legend, as the snakes coiled around him, Ragnar is said to have uttered the famous words: *"How the little piglets would grunt if they knew how the old boar suffers."* This was a clear reference to his **sons**, who would avenge his death. His final words were not a cry for mercy but a challenge—a promise of vengeance that would live on through his children.

The Revenge of Ragnar's Sons

Ragnar's death set into motion a legendary chain of events. His sons, including the famous **Ivar the Boneless**, **Bjorn Ironside**, **Sigurd Snake-in-the-Eye**, and **Ubbe**, were renowned warriors in their own right. Upon hearing of their father's death, they swore vengeance on King Ælla. In what is known as the **Great Heathen Army**, Ragnar's sons gathered a vast Viking force and launched a massive invasion of England in **865 CE**. Their campaign swept across much of Anglo-Saxon England, and eventually, they captured King Ælla, killing him in a particularly gruesome manner by performing the **blood eagle**, a legendary Viking execution method.

Ragnar's sons, each driven by the memory of their father, carved out their own legacies, establishing Viking rule across large parts of England, and continuing the cycle of conquest that Ragnar had begun. His death became a rallying point for his descendants, and through their actions, the name **Lodbrok** would be remembered for generations.

Symbolism and Cultural Impact

Ragnar Lodbrok's story is emblematic of the **Viking ethos**—a relentless pursuit of glory, conquest, and honor, even in the face of certain death. His **courage**, **craftiness**, and defiance in the face of defeat made him a legendary figure, not only among his fellow Vikings but also among the enemies who feared him. Ragnar's life represents the **heroic ideal** that the Norse deeply admired: living fearlessly, seeking out adventure, and facing one's fate with **dignity and pride**, even in death.

The image of Ragnar dying in the **snake pit**, yet remaining unbroken, is a powerful symbol of **defiance** against the odds. It highlights the Viking belief in **fate** and how death is something to be faced without fear. For the Norse, what mattered most was not the inevitability of death but how one lived and died. Ragnar's final words in the snake pit demonstrate this perfectly—he accepts his fate, but not without the knowledge that his sons will avenge him, continuing his legacy.

The saga of Ragnar Lodbrok has had a lasting cultural impact, shaping the way we view the Viking Age and its larger-than-life heroes. His story has been retold countless times in literature, art, and more recently, in popular television series, where Ragnar's legend has captured the imaginations of modern audiences. His tale is one of **adventure, ambition, and defiance**, and it stands as one of the most iconic narratives in Norse mythology.

Cultural Impact and Legacy

Ragnar's life and death encapsulate the essence of Viking ideals—conquest, honor, and the acceptance of fate. His **fearlessness in battle**, relentless ambition, and eventual

defiance in death became the archetype for the Viking warrior, influencing not just his own time but also how Viking culture has been remembered throughout history. His sons' vengeance on his behalf only solidified Ragnar's legacy, ensuring that his name would live on, not just through his deeds but also through the actions of his descendants.

Today, Ragnar Lodbrok remains one of the most well-known figures from the Viking Age, his story immortalized in both **historical sagas** and **modern media**, continuing to inspire those fascinated by the fierce spirit of the Vikings.

4.4 SUMMARY AND KEY TAKEAWAYS

Summary

In this chapter, we explored some of the most famous heroes in Norse mythology, each of whom embodied the values of bravery, loyalty, and honor. These legendary figures, immortalized in **sagas**, helped shape the cultural identity of the Norse people, blending elements of myth and history to create timeless tales of triumph and tragedy.

The Legendary Heroic Sagas

The **sagas** are the primary storytelling medium in Norse culture, blending myth with history to recount the adventures of heroes, kings, and families. These epic tales not only entertained but also preserved the cultural values of the Viking Age, illustrating how heroes were expected to navigate honor, family loyalty, and the ever-present hand of fate. The sagas present larger-than-life heroes who often face tragic endings, reflecting the Norse belief in the inevitability of fate.

Sigurd and the Dragon Fafnir

Sigurd is one of Norse mythology's greatest heroes, known for his epic battle with the dragon **Fafnir**. With the aid of his sword **Gram**, Sigurd kills the dragon and claims Fafnir's cursed treasure, including the **ring Andvaranaut**. However, the curse on the treasure ensures that Sigurd's story, despite his triumph, ends in betrayal and tragedy, as he is eventually killed by those he trusted. Sigurd's tale is a profound reflection on how even the greatest hero cannot escape the consequences of fate and greed.

Ragnar Lodbrok: Warrior-King of Legend

Ragnar Lodbrok was a legendary Viking king and warrior, renowned for his daring conquests across England and France. His raid on Paris and his many victories earned him fame and fear across Europe. However, it was his defiant death in a **snake pit**, ordered by King Ælla of Northumbria, that cemented his place in legend. Even in death, Ragnar's spirit remained unbroken, and his sons would later avenge his death, ensuring that his legacy lived on through their own triumphs.

Key Takeaways:

1. **Sagas as a Cultural Touchstone**: The **sagas** blend mythology and history to preserve the heroic deeds of Norse heroes, highlighting the values of bravery, honor, and loyalty that were essential to Viking society. Through these stories, Norse culture passed on lessons about fate, family loyalty, and the hardships of life.

2. **Sigurd's Heroism and Tragedy**: Sigurd's defeat of the dragon Fafnir represents one of the greatest feats in Norse mythology, but his story is ultimately a tragic one, demonstrating the inescapable consequences of **fate** and the curse of greed. Sigurd's life and death offer insights into the Norse view that even heroes cannot escape their destiny.

3. **Ragnar's Defiance and Legacy**: Ragnar Lodbrok's life as a conqueror and his defiant death in a snake pit exemplify the Viking ideal of facing **fate** with courage. His enduring legacy, carried on by his sons, reinforces the Norse belief in the power of family and revenge, making Ragnar an iconic figure in both history and mythology.

Reflective Questions

- How do the sagas blend historical events and mythological elements, and what does this say about the Norse view of heroism and the role of the gods in human affairs?
- Sigurd's story is a tale of both triumph and tragedy. How does the cursed treasure shape his fate, and what does this suggest about the Norse understanding of greed and destiny?
- Ragnar Lodbrok's defiant death in the snake pit symbolizes his unyielding spirit. How does his story reflect the Viking ideals of honor, bravery, and the importance of family legacy?

4.5 MYTHOLOGY QUIZ 4

Test your knowledge about the concepts and figures discussed in this chapter with the following questions:

1. **What type of creature did Sigurd slay to claim the cursed treasure?**

    A) A giant

    B) A wolf

    C) A dragon

    D) A serpent

2. **What was the name of Sigurd's sword, which he used to defeat Fafnir?**

    A) Gungnir

    B) Gram

    C) Mjolnir

    D) Skidbladnir

3. **How did Sigurd gain the ability to understand the language of birds?**

    A) By drinking from Mimir's well

    B) By tasting Fafnir's blood

    C) By wearing a magic ring

    D) By touching Yggdrasil

4. **How did Ragnar Lodbrok die, according to legend?**

    A) In battle against the Franks

    B) Killed by a giant

    C) In a snake pit

    D) Drowned at sea

5. **What did Ragnar say in his final moments to foreshadow the revenge of his sons?**

    A) "I shall return in the afterlife."

    B) "The gods will avenge me."

    C) "How the little piglets would grunt if they knew how the old boar suffers."

    D) "Odin awaits me in Valhalla."

6. **What was the name of the legendary Viking army formed by Ragnar's sons to avenge his death?**

    A) The Great Heathen Army

    B) The Berserker Brigade

    C) The Sons of Asgard

    D) The Iron Horde

Note: Answers to the quiz can be found in the "Answer Key" section in the Appendix.

CHAPTER 5:
THE UNDERWORLD
AND THE AFTERLIFE

In Norse mythology, **Hel** is both the name of a deity and the underworld realm she rules. The realm of **Hel** serves as the resting place for those who die of illness, old age, or otherwise do not fall in battle. This realm differs significantly from **Valhalla**, the hall of warriors ruled by Odin, where those who die heroically in combat are chosen by the **Valkyries** to prepare for **Ragnarok**. While Valhalla is a place of honor and preparation for battle, Hel's domain is a much more somber, quiet, and mysterious place, where the dead exist in relative stillness.

Hel's Underworld

Hel, the goddess, is the daughter of the trickster god **Loki** and the giantess **Angrboda**. She is depicted as a dark and solemn figure, with one side of her body appearing like a living woman and the other side resembling a decaying corpse, symbolizing her connection to both life and death. The realm she governs—also known as **Helheim**—is located deep in the icy, mist-covered region of **Niflheim**, far from the more familiar realms of Asgard and Midgard.

Hel's underworld is described as a cold, dark place where the souls of the dead dwell. It is not a place of punishment like the Christian concept of hell, but rather a final resting place for those who die of natural causes or without glory. The realm of Hel is vast, stretching far beyond what mortals can imagine, and is divided into various regions where the dead live out an eternal existence, largely without purpose or joy.

Unlike Valhalla, where the fallen warriors train and feast in preparation for the final battle at Ragnarok, those who reside in Hel's realm have no such purpose. They do not engage in battles or celebrations but simply exist in a state of shadowy, muted existence. The overall tone of Helheim is one of **passivity** and **isolation**, in contrast to the lively and honor-filled halls of Valhalla.

The Journey to Helheim

The journey to Helheim is depicted as a long and difficult process for the souls of the dead. In some accounts, the dead must cross the **Gjoll River** on the **Gjallarbrú** bridge, which is guarded by the giantess **Modgudr**, before reaching the gates of Helheim. Hel's realm is also protected by the fearsome hound **Garm**, who ensures that no souls escape. Once the dead pass these thresholds, they enter into the realm of Hel, where they will remain for eternity.

For many, this journey is inevitable, as the majority of people in Norse society did not die in battle. While Valhalla is reserved for the few, Helheim is the destination for the many. It represents the common fate that awaits those who die a natural death, reflecting the Norse view that not everyone can achieve a glorious afterlife.

Hel vs. Valhalla

The main difference between **Hel** and **Valhalla** lies in the **nature of the afterlife** they offer. Valhalla is a place of honor, reserved for warriors who fall in battle, where they live in grandeur, training and feasting until the day of Ragnarok. It is a place of eternal glory, where the dead are rewarded for their bravery and dedication to the gods, especially Odin.

In contrast, Helheim is a far more neutral place. It is neither a paradise nor a place of punishment, but rather a realm of the dead where those who did not die heroically reside. There is no feasting or preparation for battle in Helheim. Instead, the dead simply exist in a cold, shadowy world, far removed from the vibrancy of Valhalla. This division reflects the Norse belief that not all deaths are equal—those who die in battle are honored, while others simply move into the stillness of the afterlife.

However, Hel's realm is not entirely without significance. It is said that **Baldur**, the beloved god who was tragically killed, resides in Helheim after his death, waiting for the end of the world. His presence in Hel's realm adds a layer of depth to its meaning—it is not just a place of darkness, but also a realm that holds a crucial role in the larger cosmic order.

Symbolism and Cultural Impact

Hel and her realm represent the **inevitability of death** and the Norse understanding of the **afterlife**. While Valhalla is reserved for the elite—the warriors who fall in battle—Helheim is the resting place for the vast majority, reflecting the practical reality of death in

Norse society. It teaches that not every soul can achieve the highest honor in death, and that most will live out an afterlife of quiet isolation, just as they lived humble lives on earth.

Hel herself is a deeply symbolic figure. Her dual nature, half-living and half-dead, embodies the complex relationship the Norse had with death—accepting it as a part of life, yet always aware of its chilling finality. Her role as ruler of the underworld reinforces the notion that even the gods cannot escape the grasp of death, as evidenced by Baldur's presence in her realm.

The contrast between Helheim and Valhalla serves as a powerful reminder in Norse mythology that fate is not equal for all, and that how one dies plays a significant role in determining one's eternal destiny.

5.2 VALHALLA: THE HALL OF THE FALLEN

Valhalla, the **Hall of the Fallen**, is one of the most iconic and revered places in Norse mythology. Ruled by **Odin**, the Allfather, Valhalla serves as the afterlife for the bravest warriors who fall in battle. These chosen warriors, known as the **Einherjar**, are gathered by the **Valkyries** and brought to Valhalla, where they spend their days preparing for the ultimate battle at **Ragnarok**, the end of the world. Unlike the realm of **Hel**, where the dead exist in stillness and shadow, Valhalla is a place of **honor, glory, and eternal preparation** for the final cosmic battle.

The Hall of Warriors

Valhalla is described as a vast, majestic hall located in **Asgard**, the realm of the gods. The hall itself is a place of unimaginable grandeur, with a roof made of **shields** and walls lined with **spears**, symbolizing its warrior nature. The **Valkyries**, Odin's handmaidens, are tasked with selecting the most heroic warriors from the battlefield and bringing them to Valhalla. Only those who die bravely in combat are worthy of this honor, reflecting the Norse belief that a glorious death in battle is the most desirable end for a warrior.

Inside Valhalla, the **Einherjar** live a life of both **training** and **feasting**. During the day, they engage in fierce combat, sharpening their skills and preparing for the day when they will fight alongside Odin at Ragnarok. Every evening, after these battles, they are resurrected to join in a grand feast, where they eat the meat of the **boar Saehrímnir** and drink endless quantities of **mead** provided by the goat **Heidrun**, whose udders produce an unlimited supply of the drink. This cycle of battle, resurrection, and feasting continues day after day, ensuring that the warriors are always in peak condition when the final battle comes.

Odin's Preparation for Ragnarok

Odin's ultimate goal in gathering the bravest warriors in Valhalla is to prepare for **Ragnarok**, the prophesied end of the world, when the gods will face the forces of chaos in a final, apocalyptic battle. Odin is acutely aware of his fate—he knows that he will die at the hands of the wolf **Fenrir** during Ragnarok. However, despite this knowledge, he tirelessly prepares for the event, knowing that the Einherjar will fight alongside the gods in a last attempt to stave off destruction.

The warriors in Valhalla are not just training for personal glory; they are part of Odin's larger plan to gather an army capable of standing against the forces of chaos, led by Loki and the giants, in the battle that will determine the fate of the Nine Realms. Valhalla is a place of **preparation**, where the dead are given the opportunity to fight once more, this time for the fate of the cosmos.

Odin's role as the ruler of Valhalla also speaks to his character as the **god of war, wisdom, and fate**. While Thor protects Midgard from immediate threats, Odin is focused on the long-term battle of Ragnarok, gathering warriors and preparing strategies for the inevitable end. The Einherjar, though they live in luxury, are fully aware of their ultimate purpose: to face death again, this time in the most important battle of all.

The Role of the Valkyries

Central to the operation of Valhalla are the **Valkyries**, Odin's warrior maidens, who choose which warriors are worthy of entering Valhalla. They ride across the battlefields of Midgard, deciding the fates of men and guiding the spirits of the bravest warriors to the hall of the fallen. The Valkyries are depicted as fierce and beautiful, equally capable of fighting and guiding the dead. Their connection to both battle and the afterlife highlights their dual role as both warriors and **psychopomps**, beings who escort souls to the afterlife.

In Valhalla, the Valkyries serve as cupbearers, offering mead to the Einherjar during their nightly feasts. Their presence is a reminder of the bond between the mortal and divine, as they are the ones who ensure that the warriors selected for Valhalla are honored and cared for in the afterlife.

Valhalla vs. Helheim

Valhalla stands in stark contrast to **Helheim**, the realm ruled by Hel. While Helheim is a cold and passive resting place for those who die of natural causes or in an unremarkable manner, Valhalla is a realm of **eternal glory** for the fallen warriors. In Valhalla, the dead are not simply passive spirits, but active participants in Odin's plans for Ragnarok. The warriors in Valhalla live out an idealized version of the Viking warrior's life—fighting during the day, feasting at night, and enjoying the camaraderie of fellow warriors.

This difference reflects the **Norse cultural emphasis** on death in battle as the highest honor. While most souls go to Helheim, reserved for those who die in less heroic circumstances, Valhalla is an exclusive realm for the brave, a reward for those who live and die by the sword. The importance of Valhalla in Norse mythology underscores the warrior ethos of the Vikings, where a **glorious death** on the battlefield was seen as the most desirable way to die.

Symbolism and Cultural Impact

Valhalla represents the **Norse ideal** of honor, courage, and glory in death. For the Vikings, the concept of dying bravely in battle and being chosen for Valhalla was not just a mythological aspiration but a cultural goal. Warriors would go into battle with the hope of being chosen by the Valkyries to join the ranks of the Einherjar, living out an eternal life of honor and purpose, even after death.

The cycle of battle and resurrection in Valhalla reflects the **cyclical nature** of life, death, and rebirth that is present throughout Norse cosmology. Valhalla also represents the **inevitability of fate**. Although the warriors are preparing for Ragnarok, they know they cannot prevent it—only fight as bravely as they can when the time comes. This balance of preparation and acceptance of fate is a key theme in Norse mythology, where the gods and mortals alike strive for glory, knowing that death is ultimately unavoidable.

In modern culture, Valhalla continues to be a symbol of bravery, honor, and the pursuit of glory, influencing literature, art, and even military traditions. The concept of Valhalla has transcended its mythological origins to become a universal symbol of the afterlife as a place of honor and eternal reward for the brave.

5.3 RAGNAROK: THE END AND REBIRTH OF THE WORLD

In Norse mythology, **Ragnarok** represents both the end of the world and its rebirth, a cataclysmic series of events that will bring about the **final battle between gods and giants**, resulting in the destruction of much of the cosmos. Though Ragnarok spells doom for the gods, it is not merely an apocalypse; it is a crucial turning point in the cyclical nature of Norse cosmology, where the end of the old world paves the way for the creation of a new one.

The Prophecy of Ragnarok

The prophecy of Ragnarok begins with a period of **chaos** and **unrest**. According to myth, several key events signal the approach of this final battle. These include the **Fimbulwinter**, a harsh, endless winter that lasts for three years with no sunlight, plunging the world into darkness and despair. This long winter is marked by conflicts, family feuds, and the breakdown of moral order, with brother fighting brother.

As the Fimbulwinter draws to a close, other terrifying signs appear. The **Midgard Serpent** (Jormungandr), who lies coiled around the world, will rise from the sea, causing massive tidal waves that flood the earth. The wolf **Fenrir**, bound by the gods, will break free of his chains and begin his rampage of destruction. **Surtr**, the giant from **Muspelheim**, the realm of fire, will set the world ablaze with his flaming sword, and the sky will crack open as the giants of **Jotunheim** march upon **Asgard**.

During these events, **Heimdall**, the ever-vigilant guardian of the Bifrost, will blow the **Gjallarhorn**, a horn whose sound will echo across the Nine Realms, signaling the beginning of the final battle. The **gods**, led by Odin, will gather their forces—the **Einherjar** warriors from Valhalla—and prepare for the inevitable confrontation with the giants and the monstrous beings who rise against them.

The Final Battle: Gods vs. Giants

The battle of Ragnarok is a climactic confrontation between the **Aesir gods**, the forces of order and creation, and the **giants and monsters**, who represent chaos and destruction. Odin, knowing that this battle is unavoidable, leads the gods into the fray, but he and the other gods are aware that **fate** has already sealed their doom. Despite this knowledge, the gods face their enemies with valor, determined to fight until the end.

Each god meets their destined foe in this final battle:

- **Odin** faces the mighty wolf **Fenrir**, who breaks free of his bonds. In a fierce struggle, Odin is swallowed whole by Fenrir, fulfilling the prophecy of his death.
- **Thor** takes on his archenemy, **Jormungandr**, the Midgard Serpent. After a monumental battle, Thor slays the serpent but is poisoned by its venom. Though he takes nine steps in victory, he succumbs to the poison and dies shortly after.
- **Freyr**, the god of fertility and prosperity, fights the giant **Surtr**, but without his sword, he is no match for the fire giant and falls in battle.
- **Heimdall** and **Loki**, ancient rivals, engage in a deadly duel, where they both fatally wound each other, dying side by side on the battlefield.

As the gods fall, the forces of chaos continue their assault. **Surtr**, wielding his flaming sword, sets the world on fire, reducing Asgard, Midgard, and the Nine Realms to ashes. The earth sinks into the sea, consumed by the raging flames and floods, marking the end of the old world.

The Rebirth of the World

Although Ragnarok results in the destruction of the gods and the cosmos, it is not the ultimate end. In Norse mythology, **death and rebirth** are two sides of the same coin, and from the destruction of Ragnarok comes the promise of **renewal**. After the flames die down and the seas calm, a new world will rise from the ashes of the old.

It is foretold that **two human survivors**, named **Lif** and **Lifthrasir**, will emerge from the forests of **Hoddmimir**, having been hidden from the destruction. These two individuals will repopulate the earth, beginning a new era for humankind.

Additionally, several gods will survive or be reborn in the new world. **Baldur**, the beloved god who died before Ragnarok, will return from the underworld of **Helheim**. Alongside him will be his brother **Hodr**, who was also killed earlier. **Vidar** and **Vali**, sons of Odin, and **Magni** and **Modi**, sons of Thor, will survive the destruction and inherit the remnants of their fathers' power. Together, they will help rebuild the world and restore order.

The rebirth of the world after Ragnarok symbolizes the cyclical nature of Norse cosmology, where **destruction** and **creation** are intertwined. Though the gods and the old world fall, the cycle of life begins anew, with the promise of a fresh start for both gods and humans.

Symbolism and Cultural Impact

Ragnarok, as both an **apocalypse** and a **rebirth**, reflects the Norse belief in the **inevitability of fate** and the acceptance of death as part of the natural order. The gods, despite their immense power, are unable to escape their destiny, and even their greatest efforts to fight against the forces of chaos ultimately result in their demise. However, their willingness to face Ragnarok with **courage and honor** illustrates the Viking ideal of embracing fate, even in the face of certain doom.

Ragnarok also serves as a reminder of the **cyclical nature of existence** in Norse mythology. Just as the world must be destroyed, so too must it be reborn. This cycle of death and rebirth can be seen throughout the myths, where destruction often leads to regeneration, symbolizing the continuous renewal of life.

The tale of Ragnarok has had a profound impact on modern depictions of **apocalyptic themes** in literature, art, and film. Its themes of unavoidable doom, cosmic battles, and eventual renewal continue to resonate with audiences today, serving as a powerful metaphor for the **struggles between order and chaos**, as well as the hope for renewal after destruction.

5.4 SUMMARY AND KEY TAKEAWAYS

Summary

In this chapter, we explored the **Norse underworld** and the afterlife, focusing on the realms of **Hel** and **Valhalla**, as well as the ultimate event in Norse mythology, **Ragnarok**. These afterlife beliefs and the prophecy of the world's end reveal deep insights into the Viking views on death, honor, and the inevitable cycle of destruction and rebirth.

Hel and the Realm of the Dead

Helheim, ruled by **Hel**, is the underworld where those who die of illness or old age reside. Unlike Valhalla, it is a cold, quiet place where the dead exist in relative stillness. Helheim reflects the Norse belief that not all deaths are equal, with those who die in battle going to Valhalla while the rest go to Hel. Helheim is not a place of punishment, but rather a resting place for those who did not die in glory.

Valhalla: The Hall of the Fallen

Valhalla, Odin's hall of warriors, is reserved for those who die heroically in battle. The fallen warriors, known as the **Einherjar**, train and feast in preparation for **Ragnarok**, when they will fight alongside the gods. Valhalla is a place of honor and glory, in contrast to the stillness of Helheim. The warriors there live a cycle of battle and resurrection, awaiting the final confrontation between the forces of chaos and order.

Ragnarok: The End and Rebirth of the World

Ragnarok is the prophesied end of the world, where the gods, led by Odin, will face the giants and monsters in a final battle. Key events such as the **Fimbulwinter**, the breaking of **Fenrir's** bonds, and the rise of the **Midgard Serpent** signal the beginning of Ragnarok. Though the gods and many of the world's creatures will perish in the conflict, Ragnarok is followed by a **rebirth**, as a new world rises from the ashes, and a few gods, along with two human survivors, will continue the cycle of life.

Key Takeaways:

1. **Helheim vs. Valhalla**: Helheim is a resting place for those who die of natural causes, while Valhalla is reserved for warriors who die gloriously in battle. These two afterlife realms reflect the Norse view that a heroic death brings honor and purpose in the afterlife.

2. **The Role of Valhalla and the Einherjar**: In Valhalla, warriors train for Ragnarok, living in a cycle of **battle and feasting** under Odin's leadership. Their purpose is to fight in the final battle, demonstrating the Viking ideal of continuous preparation and bravery, even after death.

3. **Ragnarok and Rebirth**: The prophecy of Ragnarok reflects the Norse belief in the inevitability of **fate** and the **cyclical nature of life**. Despite the destruction of the gods and the Nine Realms, the world is reborn, symbolizing the endless cycle of death and renewal that underpins Norse cosmology.

The afterlife in Norse mythology is closely tied to how one dies, and the prophecy of Ragnarok shows that even in destruction, there is always the promise of a new beginning.

Reflective Questions

- How does the distinction between **Helheim** and **Valhalla** reflect the Norse understanding of **honor and glory** in death? What do these two realms tell us about the importance of dying in battle versus natural causes?
- In what ways does the **cycle of training, resurrection, and feasting** in Valhalla represent the Norse values of **eternal preparation** and **bravery**, even in the afterlife? How does this concept influence Viking ideals of courage?
- **Ragnarok** is both the end and the beginning of the world. How does the prophecy of Ragnarok illustrate the Norse belief in the **inevitability of fate** and the **cyclical nature of life**? What does the rebirth of the world after Ragnarok suggest about Norse views on destruction and renewal?

5.5 MYTHOLOGY QUIZ 5

Test your knowledge of the Norse afterlife and the prophecy of Ragnarok with the following questions:

1. **Who rules over Helheim, the realm of the dead for those who die of illness or old age?**

    A) Odin

    B) Freyja

    C) Hel

    D) Loki

2. **What type of warriors are taken to Valhalla after dying heroically in battle?**

    A) Jotnar

    B) Einherjar

    C) Valkyries

    D) Berserkers

3. **Which event signals the beginning of Ragnarok?**

    A) The fall of Yggdrasil

    B) The rise of Surtr

    C) The sounding of Gjallarhorn

    D) The defeat of Fenrir

4. **What happens to the warriors in Valhalla after their daily battles?**

    A) They are sent to Helheim

    B) They die permanently

    C) They are resurrected and feast in Odin's hall

    D) They become Valkyries

5. **Who is destined to kill Odin during Ragnarok?**

    A) Jormungandr

    B) Loki

    C) Fenrir

    D) Surtr

6. **After the destruction of Ragnarok, which two humans will survive and repopulate the earth?**

    A) Lif and Lifthrasir

    B) Thor and Sif

    C) Magni and Modi

    D) Baldur and Hodr

7. **What creature would devour the heart of those deemed unworthy in the Weighing of the Heart ceremony?**

   A) Anubis

   B) Ammit

   C) Set

   D) Bastet

Note: Answers to the quiz can be found in the "Answer Key" section in the Appendix.

CHAPTER 6:
MYTHICAL CREATURES
AND MONSTERS

6.1 FENRIR: THE MONSTROUS WOLF

One of the most fearsome and iconic creatures in Norse mythology is **Fenrir**, the **monstrous wolf** who plays a pivotal role in the events leading up to **Ragnarok**, the end of the world. Fenrir is more than just a symbol of destruction—his story embodies the tension between **order and chaos**, **fate**, and the inevitability of **doom** for the gods, particularly **Odin**.

Fenrir's Origins and Early Life

Fenrir is the son of the trickster god **Loki** and the giantess **Angrboda**, making him the brother of two other fearsome creatures: **Jormungandr**, the Midgard Serpent, and **Hel**, the ruler of the underworld. From his birth, Fenrir was destined to play a significant role in the downfall of the gods. Even as a pup, it was clear that Fenrir would grow into a powerful and dangerous beast, and the gods of **Asgard** grew fearful of his strength and potential threat.

The gods sought to control Fenrir by binding him with chains, but each time they tried, Fenrir easily broke free. Eventually, they commissioned the dwarves to create a magical chain called **Gleipnir**, made from impossible materials like the sound of a cat's footfall and the roots of a mountain. Gleipnir was light and thin, but enchanted to be unbreakable. The gods tricked Fenrir into wearing it by challenging him to break free, but Fenrir, sensing their deception, demanded one of the gods place their hand in his mouth as a show of good faith. Only **Tyr**, the god of war and justice, was brave enough to agree. When Fenrir realized he had been bound for good, he bit off Tyr's hand in anger.

Fenrir's Role in Ragnarok

The binding of Fenrir delayed his inevitable role in Ragnarok, but it could not prevent it. According to prophecy, Fenrir would eventually break free from Gleipnir during Ragnarok, joining the forces of **chaos** led by his father, Loki, and the giants. Fenrir's release marks one of the key signs that Ragnarok has begun, as his hunger and fury know no bounds.

Once freed, Fenrir will wreak havoc across the Nine Realms, bringing destruction wherever he goes. His most significant role, however, is his **confrontation with Odin**. It is foretold that during the final battle of Ragnarok, Fenrir will seek out Odin on the battlefield. Despite Odin's great wisdom and preparation, he is no match for the ferocious wolf. Fenrir will **devour Odin**, fulfilling the prophecy that the Allfather will meet his end at the jaws of the beast.

However, Fenrir's victory over Odin is not the end of his story. After slaying the king of the gods, Fenrir will be confronted by **Vidar**, Odin's son, who is prophesied to avenge his father's death. Vidar, known for his great strength and silence, will engage Fenrir in a battle to the death. Vidar, wearing a special shoe made from the scraps of leather left by shoemakers, will use his foot to pin Fenrir's lower jaw to the ground, preventing him from biting. With his immense strength, Vidar will then drive his sword into Fenrir's heart, finally killing the monstrous wolf and avenging Odin's death.

Symbolism and Cultural Impact

Fenrir's story is rich in symbolism, representing the **inevitability of fate** and the **balance between order and chaos**. Despite the gods' efforts to control him, Fenrir's role in Ragnarok is predestined, emphasizing the Norse belief that fate is unavoidable, even for the gods. His ability to break free from Gleipnir reflects the unstoppable force of chaos that the gods, despite their power, cannot hold back forever.

The story of Fenrir also reflects the **darker side of nature**, where raw power and untamed instincts cannot be controlled. As the son of Loki, Fenrir represents the destructive aspects of his father's trickster nature, but in a much more physical and brutal form. While Loki is known for his cunning and deception, Fenrir is a force of sheer **violence and destruction**.

In Norse culture, Fenrir's eventual defeat at the hands of Vidar is a reminder that, while chaos and destruction are inevitable, there will always be a response, a **balance** to the chaos. Vidar, a relatively quiet and less prominent figure in Norse mythology, plays a key role in restoring order, reflecting the belief that even in the face of great destruction, new forces will rise to restore balance.

Fenrir's presence in modern culture continues to be a powerful symbol of **uncontrollable forces**. His image as the monstrous wolf devouring Odin has become an iconic representation of the chaotic powers that eventually consume even the mightiest of rulers, reminding us of the ever-present tension between creation and destruction.

Cultural Impact and Legacy

Fenrir's story has transcended its mythological roots to become a symbol of raw, uncontrollable power. In Norse mythology, he is the embodiment of **chaos** and **destruction**, his presence a constant reminder of the inevitability of fate and the power of nature to undo even the gods' best-laid plans. His defeat at the hands of Vidar, however, demonstrates the Norse belief in **balance**—that chaos can only reign for so long before order, symbolized by Vidar's vengeance, is restored.

Fenrir's influence extends into modern depictions of **monsters and chaos** in literature, film, and art. His story serves as a powerful metaphor for the uncontrollable forces that lurk beneath the surface of even the most orderly worlds, waiting for the moment when they can break free and wreak havoc.

6.2 JORMUNGANDR: THE WORLD SERPENT

In Norse mythology, **Jormungandr**, the **World Serpent**, is one of the most fearsome and significant creatures in the cosmos. Known for his immense size, Jormungandr is said to be so large that he encircles the entirety of **Midgard** (the world of humans), biting his own tail. His presence is central to the Norse conception of the world's fate, and his role as **Thor's archenemy** sets the stage for their ultimate confrontation at **Ragnarok**, the end of the world.

Origins and the Serpent's Encircling of Midgard

Jormungandr is one of the three monstrous offspring of the trickster god **Loki** and the giantess **Angrboda**, making him the sibling of **Fenrir**, the monstrous wolf, and **Hel**, the ruler of the underworld. Early in Jormungandr's life, the gods, recognizing his immense power and potential for destruction, sought to prevent him from causing chaos. Odin, in particular, feared the creature's size and strength and cast Jormungandr into the **sea** that surrounds Midgard, hoping to keep him contained and distant from the other realms.

However, Jormungandr's growth was relentless. Over time, he grew so large that he stretched around the entirety of Midgard, eventually biting his own tail, becoming an embodiment of the **ouroboros**—a symbol of eternity, cycles, and the self-consuming nature of existence. In this form, Jormungandr became both a physical and symbolic boundary between Midgard and the other realms, representing the unbreakable connection between creation and destruction.

Thor and Jormungandr: An Ancient Rivalry

Jormungandr is best known for his enmity with **Thor**, the god of thunder and the protector of Midgard. The rivalry between Thor and Jormungandr is one of the most famous and important in Norse mythology, with their eventual confrontation being a central event of **Ragnarok**.

One of the most well-known tales involving Jormungandr and Thor occurs when Thor and several companions go on a fishing expedition with the giant **Hymir**. Thor, eager to prove his strength, uses an ox head as bait and casts his line into the sea, hoping to catch Jormungandr. When the serpent takes the bait, Thor engages in a fierce struggle, pulling the massive creature up from the depths of the sea. As Thor reels the serpent closer, he prepares to strike Jormungandr with his mighty hammer **Mjolnir**, but Hymir, terrified of the potential consequences of releasing Jormungandr, cuts the line, allowing the serpent to slip back into the ocean.

This encounter, while not their final battle, highlights the immense power of both Thor and Jormungandr and foreshadows their inevitable clash at Ragnarok. The tension between the two figures represents the cosmic struggle between **order and chaos**, with Thor standing as the defender of Midgard and Jormungandr embodying the destructive forces that threaten the stability of the world.

The Final Confrontation at Ragnarok

The prophecy of **Ragnarok** foretells that Thor and Jormungandr will meet once again in a final, cataclysmic battle. When Ragnarok begins, Jormungandr will rise from the sea, releasing his grip on his tail and causing massive floods that will devastate the world. His emergence will be one of the key signs that the end is near, as his presence signals the unraveling of the natural order.

Thor, as Midgard's protector, is destined to face Jormungandr in single combat during the chaos of Ragnarok. In their epic duel, Thor will succeed in slaying the World Serpent by striking him with Mjolnir, dealing a fatal blow. However, the victory will come at a great cost. In the moments after slaying Jormungandr, Thor will be poisoned by the serpent's venom, which will seep into his body during their battle. Though Thor will take **nine steps** in triumph, he will ultimately succumb to the venom and die, fulfilling the prophecy of his death.

This confrontation represents the ultimate clash between **order and destruction**, where even the gods cannot escape their fates. Thor's victory, though significant, is bittersweet, as his death immediately follows, signaling the end of the old world and the beginning of a new cycle in Norse cosmology.

Symbolism and Cultural Impact

Jormungandr's image as the **World Serpent** encircling Midgard reflects his role as a boundary between the realms and as a force that both contains and threatens the world. His ouroboros-like form represents the **cyclical nature of life, death, and rebirth**, a key theme in Norse mythology. The serpent's connection to the sea also ties him to the chaotic and unpredictable forces of nature, which the Norse people understood as both life-giving and destructive.

The rivalry between Thor and Jormungandr highlights the tension between **order and chaos** that is central to Norse belief. Thor, the god of thunder and protector of humanity, stands against the destructive and chaotic forces that Jormungandr embodies. Their final battle at Ragnarok represents the inevitable clash between these opposing forces, where both creation and destruction are intertwined.

Jormungandr's role in modern depictions of Norse mythology continues to resonate, especially in literature, art, and popular media. The image of the **World Serpent** encircling the earth is a powerful symbol of the boundaries between worlds, and his final battle with Thor remains one of the most iconic moments in Norse mythology. His role as both a protector and a threat reflects the complex relationship between nature and humanity in Viking culture, where the sea, like Jormungandr, was both a source of sustenance and a force of destruction.

6.3 THE VALKYRIES: CHOOSERS OF THE SLAIN

Among the most fascinating figures in Norse mythology are the **Valkyries**, whose name means "choosers of the slain." These powerful, otherworldly maidens serve **Odin**, the Allfather, and play a central role in the fate of warriors on the battlefield. The Valkyries are responsible for selecting which warriors will die in battle and which will live to fight another day. Their primary role is to gather the souls of the bravest warriors, escorting them to **Valhalla**, where they join the ranks of the **Einherjar** and prepare for **Ragnarok**.

The Role of the Valkyries

The Valkyries act as **Odin's agents** on the battlefield, guiding the course of war and death. When warriors clash in battle, the Valkyries descend, unseen by mortals, to determine the fates of those fighting. They choose the most **honorable, brave, and skilled** warriors to join the ranks of the Einherjar in Valhalla, where the fallen warriors will train and feast until the final battle of Ragnarok.

Traditionally, the Valkyries are depicted as **warrior maidens**, adorned in shining armor and mounted on horseback, riding through the skies above the battlefield. In some accounts, they are seen as both **protectors and destroyers**, influencing the outcome of battles by choosing who will fall and who will survive. Their decisions are not based on randomness or cruelty but are tied to Odin's desire to gather the greatest fighters for the final conflict between gods and giants.

The process of selection is not merely about death; it is a way for the Valkyries to bestow **honor** on those they deem worthy of Valhalla. In this sense, the Valkyries represent the **reward of bravery** and **the highest honor** a warrior can receive—an afterlife filled with endless feasts, camaraderie, and preparation for the ultimate battle.

Escorting the Souls to Valhalla

After the Valkyries select their chosen warriors, they escort the souls of the fallen from the battlefield to **Valhalla**, Odin's great hall in **Asgard**. Here, the Einherjar are welcomed into an eternal life of **glory and honor**. Valhalla is a place of both rest and preparation, where the Einherjar fight during the day and feast at night, awaiting their call to arms at **Ragnarok**.

The Valkyries themselves serve the warriors in Valhalla, bringing them **mead** and attending to them during their feasts. In this capacity, the Valkyries embody the Norse ideal of a warrior's **afterlife**—a balance of battle and leisure, of honor and reward. They ensure that the Einherjar are well cared for and that their spirits remain high as they train for their final purpose in the cosmic battle to come.

The Valkyries' role in escorting the chosen to Valhalla also connects them to the concept of **fate**. Much like the **Norns** (the weavers of fate), the Valkyries decide the destinies of men, albeit more specifically on the battlefield. They act as a direct link between the mortal world and the divine, deciding who is worthy of eternal glory.

The Valkyries in Mythology

The Valkyries appear in various Norse myths and sagas, often depicted as fierce, strong-willed women who are both beautiful and fearsome. In addition to their role on the battlefield, some Valkyries, such as the famous **Brynhildr**, play key roles in **heroic sagas**. Brynhildr's story in the **Volsunga Saga** intertwines her fate with that of the hero **Sigurd**, reflecting the Valkyries' deep connection to both war and love.

Brynhildr, like many Valkyries, is portrayed as more than just a chooser of the slain—she is a complex figure, capable of deep emotions and loyalty, as well as vengeance. Her story illustrates that while the Valkyries are primarily agents of death, they also embody a range of human and divine qualities, making them some of the most dynamic characters in Norse mythology.

The Valkyries are also tied to **Odin's wisdom** and his preparation for Ragnarok. As the **Allfather**, Odin knows that the end is inevitable, but he works tirelessly to prepare for it, gathering the strongest warriors to his side. The Valkyries act as his emissaries in this endeavor, ensuring that only the most capable warriors join the ranks of the Einherjar, thus fortifying Odin's forces for the final battle.

Symbolism and Cultural Impact

The Valkyries symbolize the **Norse warrior ethos**—a life defined by courage, honor, and the pursuit of glory in battle. Their role as **choosers of the slain** ties them to the very essence of Viking culture, where a heroic death on the battlefield was seen as the greatest achievement. The Valkyries embody the idea that only those who live and die by the sword are worthy of the eternal rewards offered in Valhalla.

In many ways, the Valkyries represent the **duality of death** in Norse mythology. On one hand, they are fierce and intimidating figures who bring death to the battlefield, but on the other hand, they are also seen as **protectors** who ensure that the bravest warriors receive their due reward. This balance of destruction and honor is central to the Valkyries' role, as they both end lives and elevate them to divine status in the afterlife.

In modern interpretations, the Valkyries have come to symbolize **strength, empowerment**, and the **fierce independence** of women. Their portrayal in literature, art, and popular culture often highlights their warrior spirit and their role as arbiters of fate, further cementing their status as iconic figures in mythology.

Cultural Impact and Legacy

The Valkyries continue to be a symbol of **honor and bravery**, representing the ultimate reward for a warrior's life lived in pursuit of **valor** and **glory**. Their presence in Norse mythology emphasizes the deep cultural connection between death and honor in Viking society, where the greatest aspiration was to be chosen by the Valkyries for eternal life in Valhalla.

Their legacy extends into modern culture, where they are often depicted as powerful and independent figures, embodying both the might and the grace of warriors. The image of the Valkyrie, whether as a chooser of the slain or a symbol of empowerment, endures as a testament to the enduring power of Norse mythology and its influence on our understanding of life, death, and honor.

6.4 THE NORNS: WEAVERS OF FATE

In Norse mythology, the **Norns** are powerful, supernatural beings who control the **destiny of all living things**, including gods and mortals alike. These three sisters—**Urd (Past)**, **Verdandi (Present)**, and **Skuld (Future)**—reside at the base of **Yggdrasil**, the great World Tree, where they tend to the tree's roots and weave the threads of fate. The Norns play a crucial role in the Norse understanding of **destiny**, acting as both creators and recorders of the inevitable paths that all beings must follow. Their role is similar to that of the **Moirai** (or **Fates**) in Greek mythology, who also govern fate and ensure that each being follows its predestined course.

The Role of the Norns in Weaving Fate

The Norns are deeply intertwined with the concept of **fate (Wyrd)** in Norse mythology. They are said to carve the destinies of gods, men, and all creatures into the **roots of Yggdrasil**, setting the course for every event in the cosmos. As they weave the threads of fate, they ensure that no one, not even the gods, can escape their preordained destiny. This idea is fundamental to Norse cosmology, where even the gods themselves, including Odin, must submit to the inescapable power of fate, particularly in regard to the prophecy of **Ragnarok**.

Each Norn represents a different aspect of time: **Urd** embodies the past, **Verdandi** represents the present, and **Skuld** symbolizes the future. Together, they ensure the continuity of life's progression. Unlike human beings, who can only live in the present and anticipate the future, the Norns have a **complete understanding of time**. They exist outside the constraints of linear existence, and their weaving reflects the cyclical and interconnected nature of fate in Norse belief.

Parallels to the Greek Fates

The Norns share many similarities with the **Moirai**, the three Fates of Greek mythology. Both the Norns and the Moirai govern destiny, and both groups consist of three sisters, each with a distinct role in shaping the flow of life. In Greek myth, **Clotho** spins the thread of life, **Lachesis** measures it, and **Atropos** cuts it, symbolizing the creation, duration, and end of life. The Norns, though less focused on life's beginning and end, also influence the entirety of existence, from the past to the future.

One key difference between the two mythological traditions is the **outlook on fate**. In Greek mythology, fate is often portrayed as

rigid and deterministic, with little room for alteration, even for the gods. In Norse mythology, while fate is equally inescapable, there is more emphasis on **facing one's destiny with courage and honor**, particularly in the face of events like Ragnarok. The gods, warriors, and mortals in Norse myth know their fate is sealed, but their **response to fate**—whether they face it with bravery or resignation—is of great importance. This nuance highlights a key element of the Viking ethos: how one faces their destiny is just as important as the destiny itself.

Symbolism and Cultural Impact

The Norns symbolize the **inevitability of fate** and the Norse belief that destiny is something to be **respected and embraced**, not feared. The Norns' control over time and events illustrates the understanding that no one, not even the gods, can alter the course set for them. This concept deeply influenced the Viking view of life and death, where one's fate was accepted, but the **courage to face it** became the ultimate measure of honor. The Norns, as figures of destiny, embody the timeless notion that while the future is fixed, the journey towards it can still be shaped by one's choices and bravery.

6.5 YMIR: THE PRIMORDIAL GIANT

In Norse mythology, **Ymir** stands as the first and most important of the **Jotnar** (giants), a primordial being whose body was used to create the world. Ymir's existence marks the beginning of time, and his role in the mythological creation story reflects the raw, elemental forces from which the cosmos was born. His death at the hands of **Odin** and his brothers represents the first cosmic struggle between **order and chaos**, setting the stage for the creation of the Nine Realms.

Ymir and the Creation of the World

According to the Norse creation myth, before anything existed, there was the primordial void known as **Ginnungagap**, flanked by the fiery realm of **Muspelheim** and the icy land of **Niflheim**. It was from the interaction of fire and ice that Ymir, the first giant, was formed. Ymir is often described as a being of immense size, his body containing the chaotic elements of creation itself. As he slept, he sweated, and from his body came the first of the giants, further populating the world with his offspring.

Ymir was not alone in this primordial chaos. Alongside him emerged the giant cow **Audhumla**, whose milk sustained him. As Audhumla licked the salty ice blocks, the first of the gods, **Buri**, emerged. Buri's descendants—**Odin**, **Vili**, and **Ve**—would eventually challenge Ymir and bring about his downfall, marking the beginning of a new era of cosmic order.

The Death of Ymir and the Birth of the Cosmos

Recognizing Ymir as a symbol of **chaos**, Odin and his brothers rose up against him. In a battle of monumental scale, they killed Ymir, and from his body, they crafted the physical world. His **flesh** became the earth, his **bones** the mountains, and his **blood** the seas and rivers. Ymir's **skull** was used to form the sky, and his **brains** were scattered to create the clouds. The cosmos itself was born from the destruction of this primordial giant, symbolizing the transformation of chaos into **order**.

This act of creation from Ymir's body signifies the shift from an unformed, chaotic existence to one shaped by the gods, with distinct realms and natural laws. However, the presence of **Jotnar** (giants) in Norse mythology persists beyond Ymir, representing the ongoing threat of chaos that constantly looms over the structured world of gods and men.

Symbolism and Cultural Impact

Ymir represents the **raw, untamed forces of nature**, embodying the chaotic potential that exists before order is established. His death at the hands of Odin and his brothers reflects the Norse belief that **creation is born from destruction**. The world, in all its complexity and beauty, is a result of the gods' ability to impose order on chaos, but the ever-present threat of the Jotnar reminds us that this balance is fragile. Ymir's legacy as the foundation of the physical world emphasizes the importance of understanding both the destructive and creative forces in Norse cosmology.

6.6 SUMMARY AND KEY TAKEAWAYS

Summary

In this chapter, we explored some of the most significant **mythical creatures and monsters** in Norse mythology, each representing forces of chaos, destruction, or fate. These creatures often serve as the ultimate adversaries to the gods, playing pivotal roles in the unfolding of cosmic events, particularly in the lead-up to **Ragnarok**.

Fenrir: The Monstrous Wolf

Fenrir, the giant wolf, is the embodiment of **chaos** and **destruction**, destined to break free and devour **Odin** during Ragnarok. Despite the gods' efforts to bind him, Fenrir's escape signals the beginning of the end, but he is ultimately killed by Odin's son, **Vidar**, bringing a measure of balance to the chaos.

Jormungandr: The World Serpent

Jormungandr, Thor's ultimate nemesis, encircles **Midgard**, embodying the cyclical nature of existence. His final confrontation with Thor during Ragnarok leads to mutual destruction, symbolizing the inevitable battle between **order and chaos**, and the end of the old world.

The Valkyries: Choosers of the Slain

The **Valkyries** are warrior maidens who select fallen heroes from the battlefield and escort them to **Valhalla**. Their role in **choosing the bravest warriors** to join Odin in preparation for Ragnarok highlights the Norse ideal of **honor in death** and the importance of glory on the battlefield.

The Norns: Weavers of Fate

The Norns, similar to the Greek Fates, control the **destiny** of all beings, including gods. Their weaving of fate represents the inescapable path that all must follow, emphasizing the Norse belief that even the gods are subject to the power of destiny.

Ymir: The Primordial Giant

Ymir, the first of the giants, symbolizes the raw, untamed forces of **creation** and **chaos**. His death by the hands of Odin and his brothers marks the transition from primordial chaos to **cosmic order**, as his body is used to create the world, showing the Norse belief in **creation through destruction**.

Key Takeaways:

1. **Chaos and Order**: Many of the mythical creatures in Norse mythology, like **Fenrir** and **Jormungandr**, represent **chaos** and the constant tension between destruction and order, often culminating in their defeat during Ragnarok. Their stories highlight the cyclical nature of Norse cosmology, where chaos is necessary for the rebirth of the world.

2. **Fate and Destiny**: The **Norns** and **Valkyries** both reflect the Norse understanding of **fate**. The Norns weave the destinies of all beings, while the Valkyries ensure that those who die bravely are chosen for Valhalla, showing the strong connection between **fate, honor, and the afterlife** in Norse culture.

3. **Creation Through Destruction**: **Ymir's** death and the use of his body to create the world symbolize the Norse concept of **creation born from destruction**. This theme is central to understanding Norse mythology, particularly in

the context of Ragnarok, where the end of the world leads to its rebirth.

The creatures and beings in Norse mythology are not just adversaries but integral to the larger cosmic balance, embodying forces that the gods must face to maintain the world's order.

Reflective Questions

- How does the conflict between creatures like **Fenrir** and **Jormungandr** and the gods reflect the Norse belief in the balance between **order and chaos**? What can their roles in Ragnarok teach us about the cyclical nature of creation and destruction in Norse mythology?
- The **Valkyries** play a crucial role in determining which warriors go to Valhalla. How does their role as **choosers of the slain** highlight the importance of **honor** and **bravery** in Norse culture, and how does it compare to modern views of heroism?
- The **Norns** and their weaving of fate demonstrate the inescapable power of destiny. In what ways does this belief in **predetermined fate** influence the way Norse heroes and gods approach their struggles, and how does it differ from other mythological or cultural views on fate?

6.7 MYTHOLOGY QUIZ 6

Test your knowledge of Norse mythical creatures and monsters with the following questions:

1. **Who is the monstrous wolf that is destined to kill Odin during Ragnarok?**

    A) Fenrir

    B) Garm

    C) Skoll

    D) Hati

2. **What creature does Thor fight during Ragnarok, resulting in both their deaths?**

    A) Fenrir

    B) Jormungandr

    C) Surtr

    D) Nidhogg

3. **What is the role of the Valkyries in Norse mythology?**

    A) Weavers of fate

    B) Protectors of Yggdrasil

    C) Choosers of the slain in battle

    D) Guardians of the Bifrost

4. **What material is used to bind Fenrir?**

   A) Chains made from iron

   B) Gleipnir, a magical chain made from impossible materials

   C) A rope spun by the Norns

   D) The roots of Yggdrasil

5. **Which of the following best describes the Norns?**

   A) Giantesses who fought in Ragnarok

   B) Maidens who ride alongside the Valkyries

   C) Beings who control the fate of gods and mortals

   D) Monsters who guard Helheim

6. **From whose body was the world created in Norse mythology?**

   A) Ymir

   B) Surtr

   C) Loki

   D) Fenrir

Note: Answers to the quiz can be found in the "Answer Key" section in the Appendix.

CHAPTER 7:
LOVE, MAGIC, AND TRAGEDY
IN NORSE MYTHS

7.1 THE LOVE OF BALDUR AND HIS TRAGIC DEATH

In Norse mythology, **Baldur**, the god of **light, purity, and beauty**, is beloved by both gods and mortals. His story is one of the most poignant in Norse myth, intertwining themes of love, **prophecy**, and **betrayal**. Baldur's tragic death marks the beginning of the events leading up to **Ragnarok**, making him a central figure in the cosmic narrative of destruction and rebirth. His story demonstrates the fragile balance between life and death, and the inevitability of fate, even for the gods.

The Prophecy of Baldur's Death

Baldur was the son of **Odin** and **Frigg**, and from the moment of his birth, he was known for his radiant beauty and kind nature. He was universally adored by the other gods, who cherished him as a symbol of peace and harmony. However, Baldur began to have disturbing **dreams** foretelling his death, dreams that caused great alarm among the gods, especially his mother, Frigg.

Desperate to protect her son, Frigg sought to prevent the prophecy from coming true. She traveled throughout the **Nine Realms**, extracting oaths from all beings and objects that they would not harm Baldur. Stones, trees, metals, animals—every element of the natural world swore an oath to do him no harm. Confident in these protections, the gods took to **mocking death** by throwing weapons and objects at Baldur, knowing that nothing could harm him. However, there was one small but crucial oversight: Frigg did not seek an oath from the seemingly insignificant **mistletoe**, believing it too small and harmless to be of any danger.

Loki's Betrayal

Loki, the trickster god, learned of this vulnerability and, as is his nature, devised a plan to exploit it. While the other gods were joyfully testing Baldur's invincibility, Loki secretly fashioned a dart made of mistletoe and approached **Hodr**, Baldur's blind brother. Under the guise of helping Hodr participate in the game, Loki handed him the mistletoe dart and guided his hand to throw it. The dart struck Baldur, and to the horror of all present, Baldur **fell dead**.

The death of Baldur sent shockwaves through **Asgard**. The gods, who had believed Baldur to be invincible, were devastated by the loss of their most beloved. His death was not just a personal tragedy for Odin and Frigg but a cosmic event that symbolized the beginning of the end. With Baldur's death, the world began to edge closer to **Ragnarok**, the twilight of the gods.

Attempts to Revive Baldur

Following Baldur's death, the gods were desperate to bring him back to life. **Hermod**, Odin's son, was sent to **Helheim**, the realm of the dead ruled by **Hel**, to plead for Baldur's return. Hel agreed, but with one condition: if every being in the Nine Realms mourned for Baldur, she would release him. The gods traveled far and wide, and indeed, all beings wept for Baldur, with one notable exception.

A giantess named **Thokk**—widely believed to be Loki in disguise—refused to mourn, sealing Baldur's fate in the realm of the dead. This final act of betrayal ensured that Baldur would remain in Helheim until after Ragnarok, when he is prophesied to return to the world of the living and help rebuild the new world.

The Symbolism of Baldur's Death

Baldur's death is a crucial moment in Norse mythology, signaling the approach of **Ragnarok** and the inevitable destruction of the current world. His fall represents the loss of innocence and beauty in the face of **chaos** and **betrayal**. Despite all efforts to protect him, Baldur's fate could not be avoided, demonstrating the Norse belief that even the most cherished lives are subject to the unyielding power of **fate**.

Loki's role in Baldur's death exemplifies his nature as both a **trickster** and a **destructive force**. While the gods sought to preserve peace and harmony, Loki brought chaos and ruin, acting as the catalyst for the tragic events leading up to Ragnarok. Baldur's death ultimately reflects the **inevitability of change**, even for the gods, and the necessity of accepting fate, no matter how painful.

Cultural Impact

Baldur's death is one of the most emotionally charged events in Norse mythology, symbolizing the **fragility of life** and the inevitability of death, even for the gods. His story resonates as a reminder of the power of fate and the importance of love and loyalty, even in the face of tragedy. Baldur's eventual return after Ragnarok also symbolizes the promise of **rebirth and renewal**, highlighting the cyclical nature of Norse cosmology. His tale has influenced countless retellings in literature and art, emphasizing the enduring themes of **loss, betrayal, and hope** that define his tragic narrative.

In Norse mythology, **Seidr** is a powerful and mystical form of **sorcery** that allows its practitioners to manipulate fate, see into the future, and alter the course of events. This form of magic plays a crucial role in the lives of both gods and mortals, acting as a bridge between the mortal world and the unseen forces that govern the cosmos. The two most notable practitioners of Seidr among the gods are **Freyja**, the goddess of love, fertility, and war, and **Odin**, the Allfather, who uses Seidr to gain wisdom and knowledge of the future.

What is Seidr?

Seidr, pronounced "say-thur," is a form of **magic** closely associated with **prophecy** and the **manipulation of destiny**. It is different from other types of magic in Norse mythology, as it often involves entering a **trance-like state** in which the practitioner can interact with spirits, communicate with the dead, or gain insight into events that have not yet occurred. Seidr could be used to influence outcomes in battle, cause harm to enemies, or alter the fate of individuals.

Seidr was primarily associated with **female practitioners**, known as **völvas** or **seiðkonur** (seeresses or sorceresses), but male practitioners, though less common, also wielded this magic. In fact, Odin himself was known to practice Seidr, though it was often considered a feminine art, which sometimes led to questions about Odin's engagement with it.

The performance of Seidr often took place in a **ritual setting**, where the practitioner would be seated on a high platform, possibly using chants, songs, or rhythmic movements to induce the trance necessary for performing magic. The practitioner would then work with **spirits** or **divine forces** to gain insight into the future or to alter fate.

Freyja: Mistress of Seidr

Among the gods, **Freyja** is the most famous practitioner of Seidr. As the goddess of love, fertility, and war, Freyja's connection to Seidr highlights her complex nature, balancing creation with destruction, and nurturing with conflict. Freyja's magic was considered so powerful that she taught Seidr to **Odin**, making her not only a master of the art but also a teacher of the gods.

Freyja's ability to **shape fate** through Seidr made her an invaluable figure among the gods. She could influence the outcomes of battles, ensure fertility and prosperity, and even manipulate love and desire. Her mastery of Seidr also connected her to the realms of **death and the afterlife**, as she could communicate with spirits and interact with the dead. This ability further reinforced her role as a goddess who straddled the line between life and death, fertility and destruction.

Odin's Use of Seidr

While Freyja is often associated with Seidr, **Odin** also became a practitioner of this sorcery. Known for his insatiable thirst for **wisdom and knowledge**, Odin sought to learn Seidr in order to gain insight into the future and to manipulate fate to protect the gods from the impending events of **Ragnarok**. His willingness to engage in what was traditionally seen as a feminine art highlights Odin's complex character, as he was willing to break social conventions in order to obtain the knowledge he desired.

Odin's use of Seidr was part of his broader quest to understand the workings of the universe. He famously sacrificed his eye for a drink from **Mimir's well**, gaining wisdom, and he hung from **Yggdrasil** for nine days and nights to learn the secrets of the **runes**. Similarly, his practice of Seidr was an attempt to influence and understand the deeper forces that governed the cosmos.

Seidr allowed Odin to see into the future and prepare for the inevitable events of Ragnarok. Despite this knowledge, Odin understood that he could not fully prevent Ragnarok, but Seidr gave him the ability to anticipate and prepare for the challenges to come. His connection to Seidr is another example of the deep **interplay between fate and free will** in Norse mythology, where even the gods must accept their ultimate destinies, but can use magic and wisdom to influence the paths leading to those destinies.

The Role of Seidr in Norse Society

Beyond the gods, Seidr also played a significant role in **Viking society**. Female seers, or **völvas**, were highly respected and often called upon by leaders to perform magic, make prophecies, or provide guidance in times of crisis. In many Viking sagas, völvas are portrayed as powerful and mysterious figures, capable of bending fate and reading the future through their sorcery. Their connection to the gods and their ability to manipulate the unseen forces of the world made them both revered and feared.

Despite its association with power, Seidr was also seen as a dangerous art, capable of causing great harm if misused. Seidr practitioners could use their abilities to **curse** individuals, create misfortune, or influence the minds of others. This darker side of Seidr highlights the dual nature of magic in Norse mythology—it could be a force for good or evil, depending on how it was used.

Symbolism and Cultural Impact

Seidr represents the **interconnectedness** of fate, magic, and the gods in Norse mythology. It emphasizes the idea that **destiny is not entirely fixed** and that powerful forces, both divine and human, can influence the course of events. Freyja's mastery of Seidr underscores her role as a goddess who controls the delicate balance between creation and destruction, life and death. Meanwhile, Odin's use of Seidr reflects his relentless pursuit of knowledge, even when it requires stepping outside of traditional gender roles or societal norms.

Seidr's influence extends into the modern imagination as well, where it is often depicted as a form of **ancient, mystical power** associated with wisdom, foresight, and control over the forces of fate. Its themes of fate, prophecy, and manipulation of the unseen continue to resonate in literature and popular culture, especially in stories that explore the boundaries between **free will** and **destiny**.

7.3 THE LOVE STORY OF FREY AND GERD

In Norse mythology, the tale of **Frey** and **Gerd** is one of the most beautiful and bittersweet love stories, demonstrating the power of love to transcend boundaries, even between gods and giants. Frey, the god of **fertility, prosperity, and sunshine**, is often associated with abundance and growth, while **Gerd**, a giantess, represents the untamed wilderness. Their love story is marked by Frey's overwhelming desire and his willingness to make a great personal **sacrifice** in order to be with the one he loves.

Frey's First Glimpse of Gerd

Frey, the son of **Njord** and the brother of **Freyja**, is a Vanir god who oversees **fertility**, **peace**, and the bounties of nature. One day, while sitting on Odin's throne, **Hlidskjalf**, Frey was able to see across the **Nine Realms**. As he gazed upon **Jotunheim**, the land of the giants, he saw the radiant **Gerd** walking in her father's courtyard. Gerd was a **giantess of unparalleled beauty**, her presence so striking that it filled Frey with an immediate and all-consuming love.

Frey was captivated by Gerd's beauty, and although she was from the race of giants—historical enemies of the gods—he could not think of anything but her. His heart was consumed with longing, and his mood darkened as his desire to be with Gerd grew unbearable. Frey became despondent, unable to eat, drink, or speak about anything else. This love was so powerful that it overwhelmed his usual joyful demeanor, and his sadness began to concern those around him.

Skirnir's Mission to Win Gerd

Frey's father, **Njord**, noticed his son's gloom and asked him what troubled him. Frey confided in his father and **Skirnir**, his loyal servant and messenger, explaining that his heart was set on Gerd and that he could not live without her. However, Frey was unable to approach Gerd himself due to the deep divide between the gods and the giants, so he enlisted the help of Skirnir to act as his emissary and plead for Gerd's hand in marriage.

Skirnir agreed to help Frey but demanded a great **price** for his service: Frey's magical sword, one of the finest weapons in Asgard. This sword, which could fight on its own and was vital in battle, was a symbol of Frey's strength and protection. Despite the significance of this weapon, Frey's love for Gerd was so overwhelming that he willingly gave it to Skirnir without hesitation, making a **sacrifice** that would eventually leave him vulnerable in future battles, particularly during **Ragnarok**.

With Frey's sword in hand, Skirnir set out for Jotunheim to find Gerd and convince her to marry Frey. Upon arriving at her father's hall, Skirnir offered her gold and precious gifts, but Gerd remained unimpressed and refused his offers. Frustrated, Skirnir resorted to threats, invoking curses and spells that would bring destruction upon her and her family. It was only after these threats that Gerd finally agreed to meet Frey, setting the conditions for their union.

The Union of Frey and Gerd

Gerd's agreement to marry Frey came with a condition: they would meet in **nine nights** in a sacred grove called **Barri**. This delay further fueled Frey's longing and impatience, as he was already deeply in love with Gerd and now had to wait for the moment when they could finally be together. Despite his sacrifice of the sword, Frey was willing to endure the wait, knowing that his love for Gerd would soon be fulfilled.

On the appointed day, Frey and Gerd met in the grove, where their love was consummated, uniting the god of fertility with the giantess of the wild lands. Their union symbolized the **balance between cultivated land and untamed nature**, reflecting the Norse belief in the interconnectedness of all things, even between beings that traditionally stand in opposition to each other.

The story of Frey and Gerd is not just a love story, but also a **metaphor for the cycle of nature**. Frey's role as a fertility god ties him to the growth of crops and the fertility of the land, while Gerd, representing the raw power of nature, brings life to the earth. Their marriage is a symbol of how civilization (represented by Frey) can harmonize with the wild, untamed forces of nature (represented by Gerd), leading to the prosperity of both.

The Consequences of Frey's Sacrifice

While Frey's love for Gerd was pure and powerful, his decision to part with his sword would later have dire consequences. During **Ragnarok**, the final battle between the gods and the forces of chaos, Frey would face the giant **Surtr**, who leads the fire giants from Muspelheim. Without his sword, Frey would be unable to defend himself properly and would fall in battle, one of many gods fated to die during the apocalypse.

Frey's willingness to give up his sword reflects the **depth of his love** and the great personal **sacrifice** he was willing to make for Gerd. It also shows the Norse view that love often comes at a cost, sometimes requiring profound sacrifice, even for the gods. Frey's story is one of both joy and tragedy—while his love for Gerd brought him happiness, it also set the stage for his eventual demise during Ragnarok.

Cultural Impact

The love story of Frey and Gerd resonates deeply with themes of **sacrifice** and the delicate balance between opposing forces, such as civilization and nature. Frey's willingness to give up his sword for the sake of love shows the **power of desire** and its ability to transcend boundaries, even those between gods and giants. Their union reflects the Norse understanding of harmony in nature and the inevitable sacrifices that love sometimes demands, making it a timeless tale of passion, vulnerability, and the interconnection of all living things.

7.4 SUMMARY AND KEY TAKEAWAYS

Summary

In this chapter, we explored the complex themes of **love, magic, and tragedy** in Norse mythology, focusing on stories that reveal the power of desire, fate, and sorcery in shaping the lives of gods and mortals alike. These tales illustrate the delicate balance between joy and sacrifice, as well as the inevitable intertwining of love and loss.

The Love of Baldur and His Tragic Death

Baldur, the god of light and beauty, was beloved by all the gods. His death, caused by the trickery of **Loki** and the fatal weakness to **mistletoe**, marked a tragic turning point for the gods and signaled the approach of **Ragnarok**. The efforts to revive Baldur failed, and his death underscored the Norse belief that even the most cherished among the gods could not escape fate.

The Magic of Seidr and Norse Sorcery

Seidr, a powerful form of Norse sorcery, allowed its practitioners to influence fate, communicate with the dead, and gain knowledge of the future. It was primarily associated with **Freyja**, the goddess of fertility and war, and **Odin**, the Allfather, who used Seidr to gain wisdom and foresee Ragnarok. This magic, though powerful, came with risks and was often seen as a practice that straddled the line between life and death.

The Love Story of Frey and Gerd

Frey, the god of fertility, fell deeply in love with the giantess **Gerd** and was willing to sacrifice his most powerful weapon—his magical sword—to win her love. Their union symbolized the harmony between **civilization and nature**, but Frey's sacrifice of his sword ultimately led to his vulnerability during Ragnarok. This story highlights the tension between love, sacrifice, and the inevitable consequences of such choices.

Key Takeaways:

1. **Fate and Inevitability**: Baldur's death and the failure to bring him back reflect the Norse belief in the **inevitability of fate**, even for the gods. No amount of love or effort can reverse what is predestined, and the looming presence of Ragnarok reinforces the idea that all things, even divine lives, are subject to the forces of fate.

2. **The Power and Risks of Magic**: The practice of **Seidr** demonstrates the potent influence that **magic and sorcery** hold in Norse mythology. Freyja and Odin's mastery of Seidr allowed them to manipulate fate and gain foresight, but the use of magic also carried great risks, blurring the lines between life, death, and destiny.

3. **Sacrifice in Love**: The love story of **Frey and Gerd** underscores the idea that love often requires **sacrifice**, sometimes at great personal cost. Frey's willingness to give up his sword for love ultimately leads to his vulnerability during Ragnarok, reminding us that passion can sometimes lead to unforeseen consequences, even for gods.

Reflective Questions

- How does the tragic death of **Baldur** reflect the Norse understanding of **fate** and the inevitable approach of **Ragnarok**? In what ways does Loki's role as a trickster shape this tragic event?
- **Seidr** allows gods like Freyja and Odin to manipulate fate and gain knowledge of the future. What does the use of Seidr reveal about the Norse views on **power, magic, and destiny**? How does it compare to other mythologies' depictions of magic?

- In Frey's love story with Gerd, he sacrifices his powerful sword to win her hand. What does Frey's willingness to make such a **sacrifice** suggest about the role of **love** and **sacrifice** in Norse mythology, and how does this choice ultimately affect his fate during Ragnarok?

7.5 MYTHOLOGY QUIZ 7

Test your knowledge of the themes of love, magic, and tragedy in Norse mythology with the following questions:

1. **What was the cause of Baldur's death?**

   A) A sword strike

   B) A mistletoe dart

   C) A curse placed by Loki

   D) An enchanted weapon

2. **Who taught Odin the magic of Seidr?**

   A) Loki

   B) Freyja

   C) The Norns

   D) Thor

3. **What did Frey sacrifice to win Gerd's hand in marriage?**

   A) His life

   B) His immortality

   C) His magical sword

   D) His throne

4. **What condition did Hel place for the resurrection of Baldur?**

    A) That all beings in the Nine Realms must weep for him

    B) That Loki must release him from a spell

    C) That Odin must sacrifice his eye

    D) That Baldur's wife must remain in Helheim

5. **What role does Seidr play in Norse mythology?**

    A) It controls the weather

    B) It allows its practitioners to manipulate fate and see into the future

    C) It is the magic that binds Fenrir

    D) It gives its user control over the sea

6. **Who refused to mourn for Baldur, ensuring that he would stay in Helheim?**

    A) Loki

    B) Surtr

    C) Thokk

    D) Skadi

Note: Answers to the quiz can be found in the "Answer Key" section in the Appendix.

CHAPTER 8:
THE LEGACY OF NORSE MYTHOLOGY

8.1 NORSE MYTHOLOGY IN ANCIENT NORDIC CULTURE

Norse mythology was more than just a collection of stories for the ancient Norse people—it was the foundation upon which **Viking society**, traditions, and values were built. These myths provided a framework for understanding the world, interpreting natural phenomena, and establishing the principles of **honor, bravery, and loyalty** that were central to their way of life. The gods, goddesses, and mythical creatures within these stories reflected the values that the Vikings held most dear, and the myths themselves were passed down through generations in both **oral tradition** and **sagas**.

Shaping Viking Society

In Viking society, the **gods and goddesses** served as **role models** for human behavior. Characters like **Odin, Thor**, and **Freyja** were revered not only for their divine power but for the traits they represented. **Odin**, the Allfather, was admired for his **wisdom, sacrifice**, and **knowledge-seeking**, teaching the Vikings the importance of leadership, strategy, and foresight. Odin's relentless pursuit of wisdom, even at great personal cost, such as sacrificing his eye or hanging himself from **Yggdrasil** to gain knowledge of the runes, symbolized the value placed on wisdom and learning, especially for leaders and warriors.

Thor, the god of thunder and protector of Midgard, embodied the values of **strength, bravery, and protection**. Vikings admired his tireless defense of the world against giants and other forces of chaos, and his stories served as a reminder that a true Viking must always be prepared to **defend their home and kin**, no matter the cost. Thor's hammer, **Mjolnir**, became a symbol of protection and was often worn as an amulet by Viking warriors.

For the Vikings, who lived in a harsh and unpredictable environment, the world of the gods was intimately connected to their own. The gods were not distant figures, but active participants in the lives of humans, influencing everything from the outcome of battles to the success of a harvest. This belief reinforced the **Viking warrior ethos**, where honor, loyalty, and bravery were prized above all else. Death on the battlefield was seen as the most honorable way to die, with the fallen being chosen by **Valkyries** to reside in **Valhalla** or **Fólkvangr**, where they would prepare for **Ragnarok** alongside Odin and Freyja.

Myth and Tradition

The myths also played a key role in **Viking traditions** and **rituals**. Religious ceremonies were often held in honor of the gods, with **blóts** (sacrifices) being made to gain their favor. Thor was frequently invoked before battles, while **Freyja** and **Frey** were honored during times of planting and harvest to ensure fertility and abundance. These ceremonies strengthened the bond between the Vikings and their gods, reinforcing the idea that maintaining a good relationship with the divine was essential for both personal success and the well-being of the community.

The **cycle of life, death, and rebirth**, as reflected in myths like **Ragnarok**, mirrored the Vikings' understanding of the natural world. The changing of the seasons, the tides, and the stars were seen as part of this cosmic cycle, and the myths helped the Vikings make sense of the world around them. For example, **Yggdrasil**, the World Tree, served as a symbol of the interconnectedness of all things, with its branches extending into every realm. This idea of interconnectedness reinforced the Vikings' belief that their actions had consequences beyond their immediate lives, affecting their **afterlife** and the cosmic balance.

Values of Honor and Fate

One of the most central concepts in Norse mythology, and by extension Viking society, was the belief in **fate**. The **Norns**, the weavers of fate, controlled the destinies of gods and men alike, and their power was unchangeable. This belief in a predetermined fate shaped the Viking approach to life—**accepting one's destiny** with **bravery** and **honor** was paramount. While fate was inescapable, how a person faced it—whether with fear or with courage—defined their character.

Vikings, especially warriors, embraced this belief in fate, seeing it as an opportunity to **prove their worth**. To die with honor was the ultimate goal, as it would ensure a place in the halls of Valhalla or

Fólkvangr. This warrior ethos, deeply rooted in Norse mythology, permeated all levels of Viking society, from the leaders to the common folk, encouraging them to live bold, honorable lives.

Cultural Legacy

The influence of Norse mythology extended far beyond the realm of religion and personal values. It shaped **law, governance**, and **social structure** in Viking communities. Kings and chieftains often traced their lineage back to the gods, particularly Odin, as a way to legitimize their rule. Laws were often believed to be divinely inspired, and disputes were sometimes settled through **combat or trial by ordeal**, with the belief that the gods would ensure justice.

Norse mythology also had a profound impact on **art and storytelling**. The sagas and **Eddas**, which recorded the tales of gods, heroes, and legendary battles, were central to the Viking tradition of storytelling. These stories were not just entertainment; they were a way of **preserving history, culture, and values**. The themes of bravery, loyalty, and the inevitable confrontation with fate resonated deeply with the Viking worldview and continue to influence modern interpretations of Norse culture.

Cultural Impact

Norse mythology's influence on Viking society was all-encompassing, shaping their **beliefs, values**, and **traditions**. It provided a structure for understanding life, death, and the cosmos, and it deeply influenced the way Vikings conducted themselves in battle, worship, and governance. The values of **bravery, honor, loyalty, and the acceptance of fate** were at the core of their culture, and these ideals were reflected in their myths, ensuring that Norse mythology remains a lasting testament to the Viking way of life.

8.2 THE INFLUENCE OF NORSE MYTHS ON MODERN CULTURE

Norse mythology's influence on modern culture is vast and far-reaching, particularly in **fantasy literature**, **comics**, **music**, and **philosophy**. These ancient myths have become a key part of global popular culture, inspiring generations of creators to reimagine their themes of **heroism, fate, and cosmic conflict**.

In **literature**, J.R.R. Tolkien's works, such as *The Lord of the Rings* and *The Silmarillion*, draw directly from Norse sources. Tolkien's **dwarves**, for example, are heavily influenced by the dwarves of the **Poetic Edda**, while his **elves** and the epic battle between **good and evil** resemble the cosmic conflicts found in **Norse sagas**. Tolkien was deeply influenced by Norse concepts of **honor, fate, and courage**, which are reflected in his characters' struggles.

Comics and superhero films have also embraced Norse mythology, with Marvel's **Thor** becoming one of the most iconic characters in the **Marvel Cinematic Universe (MCU)**. Marvel's Thor has brought elements of Norse myth—such as **Mjolnir**, the **Bifrost**, and Ragnarok—to a global audience, blending them with superhero narratives. While Marvel's adaptation takes liberties with the source material, it retains core themes of Norse myth, such as the conflict between gods and giants.

Moreover, Norse mythology has influenced modern discussions around **fate and destiny**, particularly in the context of philosophical and literary debates about **free will** versus **predetermined fate**. The **Norns**, who weave the fates of gods and men, have become symbols of this larger human concern.

Cultural Impact

Norse mythology has not only shaped the **fantasy genre**, but it has also found its way into **music, philosophy, and global popular culture**, demonstrating how ancient myths can resonate with modern audiences. From **Tolkien** to **Marvel**, Norse myths have inspired new generations to explore the timeless questions of **fate, heroism, and power**.

8.3 MODERN INTERPRETATIONS AND ADAPTATIONS

Norse mythology has experienced a cultural revival in recent decades, with **modern interpretations and adaptations** of its gods, heroes, and myths permeating **TV shows, movies**, and **popular media**. Creators have reimagined these ancient stories for new audiences, blending mythology with contemporary themes and modern aesthetics. These adaptations range from faithful retellings of Norse legends to bold reworkings that bring the gods into modern settings. Through these works, Norse mythology continues to evolve, remaining a relevant and influential part of today's cultural landscape.

TV Shows: Mythology in a New Light

One of the most notable recent TV series that brought Norse mythology to a mainstream audience is **Vikings** (2013–2020). This historical drama, created by **Michael Hirst**, blends Viking history with Norse mythological themes, following the legendary hero **Ragnar Lothbrok** and his descendants. While the show primarily focuses on historical events, it incorporates mythological elements throughout. Characters often experience visions of the gods, particularly **Odin**, who appears to Ragnar and others as a guiding but mysterious figure. The Viking warriors' belief in **Valhalla** and their pursuit of an honorable death on the battlefield are central themes, reflecting the importance of Norse afterlife beliefs in their daily lives.

Another popular TV series, **American Gods** (2017–2021), adapted from **Neil Gaiman's** novel, presents a modern take on Norse mythology. In the show, **Odin** appears as "Mr. Wednesday," a scheming, manipulative figure determined to rally the old gods in a battle against the new gods of technology and media. **Loki** also makes an appearance, further connecting the modern world to ancient myth. Gaiman's interpretation of Norse gods as flawed, fading figures navigating the contemporary world offers a fresh perspective on their enduring relevance and complexity.

The Almighty Johnsons (2011–2013), a New Zealand TV series, provides a humorous twist on Norse mythology by reimagining the Norse gods reincarnated in modern human form. The Johnson brothers, who are the human incarnations of various Norse gods, must navigate their divine responsibilities while dealing with everyday life in the 21st century. The series plays with themes of fate, identity, and the burdens of power, showing how the ancient gods' influence can be adapted to fit modern narratives.

Movies: Norse Gods on the Big Screen

Perhaps the most recognizable modern adaptation of Norse mythology on the big screen comes from the **Marvel Cinematic Universe (MCU)**, where **Thor, Loki, Odin**, and other Norse figures are reimagined as superheroes. The Marvel films, starting with *Thor* (2011) and culminating in *Thor: Ragnarok* (2017) and *Avengers: Endgame* (2019), have introduced these mythological figures to a global audience in new and creative ways. While Marvel's interpretation diverges significantly from the original myths, it retains the essential elements of Thor's struggle with his brother Loki, Odin's wisdom, and the apocalyptic threat of Ragnarok.

Thor: Ragnarok (2017), directed by **Taika Waititi**, draws heavily from the myth of Ragnarok, the end of the world in Norse mythology. Though the film injects a great deal of humor and action, it still touches on the themes of destruction and rebirth, which are central to the original myth. **Hela**, the goddess of death in the movie (loosely based on the mythological **Hel**), wreaks havoc on Asgard, leading to its destruction and the survival of its people. The film showcases how Norse myths can be adapted to fit a **modern superhero narrative** while retaining core mythological elements.

In addition to Marvel, Norse mythology has been explored in other films such as **Valhalla Rising** (2009), directed by **Nicolas Winding Refn**. This dark, atmospheric film draws on Norse symbolism and explores themes of survival, fate, and violence through the journey of a mute warrior named **One-Eye**. Though more abstract in its storytelling, the film captures the bleak and rugged world of the Norse and taps into the mythological undercurrents of fate and destiny.

Another recent adaptation, **The Northman** (2022), directed by **Robert Eggers**, takes a more historical and mythologically accurate approach to Viking life and beliefs. The film, loosely based on the **Amleth** legend (a precursor to Shakespeare's *Hamlet*), incorporates Norse rituals, visions of **Valkyries**, and the brutal realities of Viking life, while also portraying the belief in fate and the gods as integral to the characters' motivations. The blend of mythology and historical accuracy offers a gritty, immersive look into how the Norse viewed their world.

Modern Mythology in Video Games

Norse mythology has also found fertile ground in the realm of **video games**, with several prominent titles drawing on its themes and characters. One of the most successful examples is **God of War** (2018), which reboots the Greek mythology-based franchise and places its protagonist, **Kratos**, in the world of Norse myth. In this game, players interact with key figures from Norse mythology, such as **Baldur**, **Freya**, and **Jormungandr** (the World Serpent). The game takes great care in portraying these characters in a manner that respects their mythological origins while weaving them into a compelling narrative about fatherhood, loss, and revenge. The upcoming sequel, *God of War: Ragnarok* (2022), promises to further explore the Norse apocalypse and the epic clash between gods and giants.

Another recent success is **Assassin's Creed: Valhalla** (2020), which immerses players in the world of the Vikings and incorporates mythological elements such as visions of **Asgard**, **Odin**, and encounters with the **Norns**, the weavers of fate. The game blends Viking history with Norse mythology, allowing players to experience the beliefs and customs of the Norse people while also engaging with their legendary gods and creatures.

Reimagining Myths: Norse Gods in Modern Fiction

Modern literature has also embraced Norse mythology, with authors reinterpreting these ancient tales for contemporary audiences. **Neil Gaiman's** *Norse Mythology* (2017) is a faithful retelling of the myths in a modern voice, capturing the essence of the original stories while making them accessible to readers unfamiliar with the Eddas. Gaiman's work has brought the Norse gods back into the literary spotlight, preserving their mythic grandeur while offering fresh insights into their personalities and relationships.

In **Rick Riordan's** *Magnus Chase and the Gods of Asgard* series, the Norse gods are reimagined in a contemporary urban setting, much like Riordan's previous work with Greek and Roman mythology in the *Percy Jackson* series. Riordan's lighthearted approach introduces younger readers to the world of **Thor, Loki, and Odin**, blending humor with the epic scope of Norse mythology.

Norse mythology in poetry and music has also thrived, particularly within the **Viking metal** subgenre of heavy metal music, where bands like **Amon Amarth** and **Bathory** draw heavily on Norse themes, singing of **Odin**, **Thor**, and the final battle of Ragnarok. These bands channel the raw energy and epic storytelling of the myths into their music, creating an auditory experience that celebrates Norse heritage.

Cultural Impact

Modern interpretations and adaptations of Norse mythology continue to shape how we engage with these ancient tales, bringing them into the mainstream through **TV shows, movies, video games, and literature**. Whether through the superhero lens of Marvel's **Thor**, the dark reimagining of Viking life in *The Northman*, or the immersive narratives of video games like **God of War**, Norse mythology has found new life in the 21st century. These adaptations preserve the essence of the myths while exploring their relevance to contemporary themes of **fate, power, and identity**, ensuring that the stories of Odin, Thor, Loki, and the rest of the Norse pantheon remain as impactful today as they were over a thousand years ago.

8.4 SUMMARY AND KEY TAKEAWAYS

Summary

In this chapter, we explored the **legacy of Norse mythology**, focusing on how these ancient stories have shaped **Viking society** and how they continue to influence **modern culture** through various adaptations and interpretations. From the gods and heroes who inspired Viking values to their enduring presence in today's **literature, movies, TV shows, and video games**, Norse mythology remains a powerful cultural force.

Norse Mythology in Ancient Nordic Culture

The myths of gods like **Odin, Thor**, and **Freyja** were more than just stories; they were the foundation of **Viking society** and shaped values such as **bravery, honor, and loyalty**. These myths guided daily life, battle ethics, and religious rituals, reinforcing the idea that **fate** governs all, even the gods. The concepts of honor in death and preparation for **Ragnarok** underscored the Viking warrior ethos, while mythological figures provided models for leadership, protection, and wisdom.

The Influence of Norse Myths on Modern Culture

Norse mythology has left a lasting mark on **modern culture**, particularly through works like **J.R.R. Tolkien's** *The Lord of the Rings*, which draws heavily on Norse myth for its characters, themes, and world-building. **Marvel's Thor**, with its cinematic universe, has brought Norse gods to new generations, blending mythology with the superhero genre. Modern video games like **God of War** and **Assassin's Creed: Valhalla** continue to explore these myths, bringing players into immersive worlds shaped by Norse legend.

Modern Interpretations and Adaptations

Norse mythology has been reinterpreted and adapted in **TV shows**, such as **Vikings** and **American Gods**, which explore the gods in both historical and modern settings. **Movies** like *Thor: Ragnarok* and *The Northman* retell these myths with contemporary twists, while **authors** like **Neil Gaiman** and **Rick Riordan** reimagine the gods in accessible and engaging ways for readers of all ages. The myths have also found a place in **music**, particularly in the **Viking metal** subgenre, where themes of Norse gods and epic battles continue to resonate.

Key Takeaways:

1. **Cultural Foundations:** Norse mythology deeply influenced Viking society, shaping their values of bravery, honor, and fate. The gods were seen as role models, and the myths reinforced the importance of courage, sacrifice, and preparing for the inevitable challenges of fate, including Ragnarok.

2. **Enduring Influence:** The stories of Norse mythology continue to influence modern culture, from literature like Tolkien's Middle-earth to movies and comics like Marvel's Thor. These adaptations preserve the core themes of Norse myths while bringing them to new generations in exciting and accessible ways.

3. **Modern Adaptations:** Through TV shows, movies, video games, and literature, Norse mythology has been reimagined for contemporary audiences. These adaptations explore themes of fate, power, and identity, showing how the ancient myths remain relevant in modern storytelling and entertainment.

Norse mythology's continued presence in modern culture ensures that the timeless stories of gods, heroes, and mythical creatures will be told for generations to come, reflecting the enduring power of these ancient legends.

Reflective Questions

- How did the values and traditions derived from Norse mythology shape **Viking society**, particularly in terms of their views on **fate, honor, and the afterlife**?
- In what ways have modern adaptations of Norse mythology, such as **Marvel's Thor** or **J.R.R. Tolkien's** works, changed or preserved the original themes and characters of the myths? What effect does this have on our understanding of these ancient stories?
- How do the reimaginings of Norse gods and myths in **video games**, **TV shows**, and **movies** reflect contemporary concerns about **identity, power, and destiny**, and why do these themes continue to resonate with modern audiences?

8.5 MYTHOLOGY QUIZ 8

Test your knowledge of the legacy and modern adaptations of Norse mythology with the following questions:

1. **Which famous fantasy author drew heavily on Norse mythology, especially for his depiction of dwarves and themes of fate?**

   A) George R.R. Martin

   B) J.R.R. Tolkien

   C) Neil Gaiman

   D) Rick Riordan

2. **In the Marvel Cinematic Universe, who is Thor's primary adversary, known for his trickery and mischief?**

   A) Hela

   B) Loki

   C) Surtr

   D) Fenrir

3. **Which recent video game features Kratos, a former Greek god, entering the world of Norse mythology and encountering gods like Baldur and Freya?**

   A) Assassin's Creed: Valhalla

   B) God of War

   C) The Witcher 3

   D) Skyrim

4. **What central theme in Norse mythology is explored in Vikings, where characters strive to gain entry to Valhalla through their actions on the battlefield?**

   A) Destiny and revenge

   B) Courage and honor in death

   C) Magic and prophecy

   D) Love and betrayal

5. **American Gods, a modern TV show based on a novel, features which Norse god disguised as "Mr. Wednesday"?**

   A) Thor

   B) Odin

   C) Loki

   D) Tyr

6. **In *Thor: Ragnarok* (2017), what event from Norse mythology does the movie depict, involving the destruction of Asgard and the end of the world?**

A) The Twilight of the Gods

B) Ragnarok

C) The Battle of Bifrost

D) The Fall of Yggdrasil

Note: Answers to the quiz can be found in the "Answer Key" section in the Appendix.

CHAPTER 9:
THE ENDURING LEGACY
OF NORSE MYTHOLOGY

Norse mythology has left an indelible mark on the world, inspiring countless generations of **storytellers, adventurers,** and **historians** alike. These ancient tales, passed down through sagas and poems, have not only survived but thrived in modern culture, proving their timelessness. The stories of gods, giants, and heroic mortals continue to resonate because they touch on fundamental themes that transcend time: **fate, honor, love, sacrifice, and the eternal battle between chaos and order**. Through literature, art, and popular media, Norse mythology remains a **living tradition**, fueling the imaginations of creators and scholars today.

Storytellers and Modern Myth-Makers

One of the most enduring aspects of Norse mythology is its ability to inspire modern storytellers. These myths have provided a fertile ground for **authors, screenwriters,** and **artists** to explore complex narratives and timeless themes. Whether it's through the retelling of the myths in contemporary settings or reimagining the gods as modern heroes and anti-heroes, Norse mythology has sparked new stories while maintaining its ancient roots.

Fantasy literature, for example, owes much to Norse mythology. Authors like **J.R.R. Tolkien** and **Neil Gaiman** have drawn deeply from the well of Norse legends. Tolkien's *The Lord of the Rings* echoes the themes of **Ragnarok**, with its portrayal of a cataclysmic battle between good and evil, and characters who face their doom with bravery and resilience. Meanwhile, Gaiman's *Norse Mythology* offers readers a modern, accessible retelling of the original myths, keeping the humor, tragedy, and grandeur of the old stories intact.

In **film and television**, the gods and creatures of Norse mythology continue to find new life. The **Marvel Cinematic Universe** (MCU) has redefined Thor, Loki, and Odin for new generations, while shows like **Vikings** and **American Gods** explore the relationship between history, myth, and modernity. Each adaptation brings something new to the myths, whether it's through humor, as in *Thor: Ragnarok*, or through deep philosophical questions about belief and power, as in *American Gods*. These stories are not mere retellings; they are **reinventions** that breathe new life into ancient characters, showing their relevance in today's world.

Adventurers: Norse Mythology as a Source of Inspiration

The adventurous spirit of the Vikings, immortalized in their myths, continues to inspire those who seek to **explore the world** and push the boundaries of what is possible. **Viking explorers** like **Leif Erikson**, who is said to have reached North America centuries before Columbus, were driven by the same courage and thirst for discovery that permeates the myths of Thor's battles and Odin's quests for wisdom.

Today, **adventure seekers** draw inspiration from the **Viking ethos** of bravery, exploration, and resilience. The idea of **facing one's fate head-on**, regardless of the outcome, has become a popular theme in adventure literature and media. In video games like **Assassin's Creed: Valhalla**, players step into the boots of a Viking warrior, navigating a world where the gods, fate, and the natural elements intertwine. These games, while rooted in historical settings, are infused with **mythological themes**, making the player's journey feel epic, as if they are walking in the footsteps of ancient adventurers.

Similarly, **outdoor enthusiasts** and **explorers** often invoke the spirit of the Vikings in their quests, whether scaling mountains or embarking on perilous journeys. The **symbolism of Thor's hammer** as a protective amulet has persisted into modern times, with many adventurers wearing it as a sign of strength and resilience.

Historians and Scholars: Unlocking the Mysteries of the Past

The fascination with Norse mythology extends beyond the world of fiction and adventure. For **historians** and **archaeologists**, the ancient texts and artifacts associated with Norse myth offer valuable insights into the **belief systems** and **societal structures** of the Viking Age. **Scholars** continue to study the **Poetic Edda**, the **Prose Edda**, and the sagas, seeking to understand how the Norse people viewed the world around them.

The gods and myths of the Vikings weren't just stories—they were a **blueprint** for how to live in a world full of unpredictability and danger. **Odin's** quest for wisdom, **Thor's** defense of Midgard, and **Freya's** balance of love and war all reflect aspects of Viking life, from the importance of knowledge and bravery to the roles of women and the power of nature. Historians and scholars continue to explore these layers, revealing how **mythology shaped Viking laws, rituals, and social practices**.

Archaeological discoveries have also shed light on how these myths were embedded in daily life. From **burial mounds** designed to emulate the idea of the afterlife in **Valhalla** to **rune stones** that commemorate battles or fallen warriors, the **physical evidence** of Norse beliefs can still be found throughout Scandinavia and beyond. These findings help historians piece together a more complete picture of how Norse mythology influenced the **cultural identity** of the Vikings and their descendants.

Enduring Lessons from Norse Mythology

At the heart of Norse mythology is the idea that **fate cannot be escaped**, but it can be faced with **courage** and **honor**. The myths teach us that, while **chaos** is inevitable—embodied in figures like

Loki and the looming threat of **Ragnarok**—what matters is how we respond to it. This lesson remains relevant in the modern world, where uncertainty and upheaval are constant forces.

The enduring legacy of Norse mythology lies in its ability to **speak to universal human experiences**. The gods and heroes of these myths face **loss, betrayal, love, and sacrifice**, much like we do today. Their stories remind us that while we may not have control over our fate, we can choose how to meet it—with **bravery, wisdom, and resilience**.

As long as these themes continue to resonate with people, Norse mythology will live on, inspiring storytellers, adventurers, and scholars to explore new ways to connect the ancient world with the present. These myths have been passed down for centuries, evolving with each generation, and will likely continue to inspire new interpretations for many years to come.

Cultural Impact and Legacy

The enduring legacy of Norse mythology is reflected in its timeless themes of **fate, courage, and sacrifice**, which continue to inspire modern creators and thinkers. From the adventurers who channel the spirit of the Vikings to the scholars who unlock the secrets of the sagas, Norse mythology remains a **living tradition**. It serves as a reminder that even in the face of chaos and uncertainty, the way we meet our fate defines our legacy.

ACKNOWLEDGMENTS

As we come to the end of this exploration of **Norse mythology**, I want to take a moment to express my gratitude to those who have contributed to the creation of this book. Delving into the world of the **Norse gods, heroes, and mythical creatures** has been an enriching experience, much like the journeys I undertook with **Greek** and **Egyptian mythology**. Each tradition has offered unique insights into how ancient cultures made sense of the world, and it has been a true privilege to share these powerful stories with you.

I extend my deepest thanks to the many **scholars, researchers, and enthusiasts** whose work laid the foundation for this book. Your passion for preserving and interpreting the myths of the Norse world has allowed me to bring these timeless tales to life. The parallels and contrasts between **Norse, Greek, and Egyptian** mythology have been fascinating to explore, showing how these cultures, though separated by time and geography, touched on similar themes of **creation, heroism, and fate**.

I am equally grateful to the **readers** who have traveled with me through these mythological worlds. Your curiosity and engagement continue to inspire me. After journeying together through **Greek** and **Egyptian** myths, it has been a true honor to dive into the heroic sagas and cosmic battles of the **Norse gods**. I hope these stories have sparked the same sense of wonder in you as they have in me.

Finally, I would like to thank my **family and friends** for their constant support and encouragement throughout this process. Whether by sharing ideas or offering feedback, your contributions have been invaluable. The preservation and telling of these ancient stories would not have been possible without you.

As we close this chapter on Norse mythology, I hope the stories of **Odin, Thor, Loki, Freyja**, and the other Norse deities will continue to resonate with you, just as they have with generations before. I look forward to more adventures in mythology, and I hope you'll join me again as we explore more tales that have shaped cultures and inspired imaginations throughout history.

Your Feedback is Valued

If this exploration of Norse mythology has resonated with you, I would be truly grateful if you could take a moment to share your thoughts by leaving a review. Your feedback not only helps others discover these legendary tales but also supports the continued sharing of these ancient stories. Thank you for being a part of this mythological journey.

ALSO BY ETHAN CRAFTWELL

Greek Mythology for Beginners: Enchanting and Timeless Tales of Gods, Heroes, and Monsters. Unveil the Secrets of Ancient Legends and Explore the Stories that Defined History.

Egyptian Mythology for Beginners: Discover the Mystical World of Gods, Heroes, Monsters and the Book of the Dead. Unveil the Secrets of Ancient Egypt and Dive into Stories that Shaped Civilization.

APPENDIX

GLOSSARY OF TERMS

Aesir
The primary group of gods in Norse mythology, including figures like **Odin**, **Thor**, and **Frigg**. They reside in **Asgard** and are associated with power, war, and governance.

Alfheim
The realm of the **light elves**, ruled by **Frey**, a god associated with fertility and peace. The elves are known for their connection to nature and magic.

Asgard
One of the Nine Realms, home to the **Aesir** gods. Connected to Midgard by the **Bifrost** (rainbow bridge), it is ruled by **Odin**.

Baldur
The god of light, beauty, and purity, beloved by all the gods. His tragic death, orchestrated by **Loki**, marks the beginning of the events leading to **Ragnarok**.

Bifrost
The rainbow bridge that connects **Asgard** (the realm of the gods) to **Midgard** (the realm of humans). It is guarded by **Heimdall**.

Einherjar
The spirits of brave warriors who have died in battle and are chosen by the **Valkyries** to reside in **Valhalla**, where they prepare for the final battle at **Ragnarok**.

Freyja
A Vanir goddess associated with love, fertility, war, and magic. She is a master of **Seidr** (Norse sorcery) and is often depicted as both a nurturing and fierce figure.

Fenrir
A monstrous wolf, the offspring of **Loki**. Fenrir is destined to kill **Odin** during **Ragnarok** but will be slain by Odin's son **Vidar**.

Ginnungagap
The primordial void that existed before the creation of the world. It lies between the fiery realm of **Muspelheim** and the icy realm of **Niflheim**.

Helheim
The realm of the dead, ruled by **Hel**, daughter of **Loki**. It is where those who die of sickness or old age dwell, unlike the warriors who go to **Valhalla**.

Jormungandr
The World Serpent, another offspring of **Loki**. Jormungandr encircles **Midgard** and is destined to battle **Thor** during **Ragnarok**, resulting in both their deaths.

Jotunheim
The land of the **giants** (Jotnar), representing chaos and destruction. It is frequently in conflict with Asgard, the realm of the gods.

Loki
The trickster god, known for his cunning and mischief. Though he helps the gods on many occasions, Loki is also responsible for many of their woes, including the death of **Baldur**. He plays a key role in the lead-up to **Ragnarok**.

Midgard
The realm of humans, located at the center of the Nine Realms. It is connected to **Asgard** by the **Bifrost** bridge.

Mjolnir
The magical hammer wielded by **Thor**, capable of summoning lightning and protecting both the gods and humans from giants and other threats.

Muspelheim

The fiery realm of **Surtr** and the fire giants. It stands in opposition to Niflheim, representing heat and chaos, and plays a crucial role in **Ragnarok**.

Niflheim

The realm of **ice** and **cold**, representing stasis and death. It is home to **Hvergelmir**, the wellspring of rivers, and lies to the north of the primordial void, **Ginnungagap**.

Norns

The three female beings—**Urd (Past)**, **Verdandi (Present)**, and **Skuld (Future)**—who control the fate of gods and men. They weave the threads of fate at the roots of **Yggdrasil**, the World Tree.

Odin

The Allfather and ruler of the **Aesir**, associated with wisdom, war, and death. Odin sacrifices greatly in pursuit of knowledge, including giving up an eye for wisdom and hanging himself from **Yggdrasil** to gain the runes.

Ragnarok

The prophesied end of the world, a cataclysmic battle between the gods (led by **Odin**) and the giants (led by **Loki** and **Surtr**), resulting in the death of many gods and the destruction of the cosmos, followed by its rebirth.

Seidr

A form of Norse sorcery associated with prophecy, fate manipulation, and magic. Practiced by **Freyja** and later **Odin**, Seidr allows its users to communicate with spirits and shape destiny.

Svartalfheim

Also known as the realm of **dwarves** or dark elves. These master craftsmen are responsible for creating many powerful artifacts, including **Mjolnir**, Thor's hammer.

Thor

The god of thunder, lightning, and storms, and protector of **Midgard**. He is known for his immense strength and his role in defending the gods and humans from giants, often wielding his hammer **Mjolnir**.

Valhalla

Odin's hall in **Asgard**, where the souls of warriors who die heroically in battle, chosen by **Valkyries**, reside. There, they prepare for the final battle of **Ragnarok**.

Valkyries

Warrior maidens who serve **Odin**. They select fallen warriors from the battlefield and bring them to **Valhalla** to join the **Einherjar**.

Vanir

A group of gods associated with fertility, prosperity, and nature, distinct from the **Aesir**. After a war between the two groups, the Vanir and Aesir formed an alliance, with **Freyja**, **Frey**, and **Njord** being prominent Vanir figures.

Vanaheim

The realm of the **Vanir gods**, who are associated with fertility, nature, and prosperity. Vanaheim plays a crucial role in maintaining the cosmic balance.

Yggdrasil

The World Tree that connects the Nine Realms. Its roots and branches extend throughout the cosmos, and it is central to Norse cosmology. The **Norns** reside at its base, weaving the fate of gods and men.

RECOMMENDED READING

For those looking to further explore Norse mythology, its rich history, and cultural significance, the following resources provide a wealth of knowledge and insight. Whether you are interested in original sources, modern retellings, or scholarly analyses, these books will help deepen your understanding of the ancient Norse world.

Primary Sources:

The Poetic Edda
Translated by Carolyne Larrington
This collection of Old Norse poems is one of the most important primary sources of Norse mythology. It contains many of the myths about gods like Odin, Thor, and Loki, as well as heroic sagas like those of Sigurd the Dragon Slayer. Larrington's translation is accessible and preserves the beauty of the original texts.

The Prose Edda
Written by Snorri Sturluson, Translated by Jesse Byock
This medieval text, written by Icelandic historian Snorri Sturluson, provides a prose version of many key Norse myths. It is an invaluable source for understanding how the Norse people viewed their gods and the structure of the cosmos. Byock's translation makes it easy to follow, even for those new to the myths.

Heimskringla: History of the Kings of Norway
by Snorri Sturluson
Another important work by Snorri Sturluson, the *Heimskringla* recounts the sagas of Norwegian kings, blending history and mythology. This text provides a fascinating look at how the Norse people intertwined their understanding of divine figures with their historical rulers.

Scholarly Works:

The Viking Spirit: An Introduction to Norse Mythology and Religion
By Daniel McCoy
A well-researched yet accessible introduction to Norse mythology and Viking religion. This book explores the major gods, themes, and stories in Norse mythology, offering historical context and cultural insights.

Norse Mythology: A Guide to Gods, Heroes, Rituals, and Beliefs
By John Lindow
This scholarly work provides a comprehensive overview of Norse mythology, including detailed descriptions of gods, creatures, and key myths. It's a must-read for those seeking a thorough understanding of the subject.

Modern Retellings and Adaptations:

Norse Mythology
By Neil Gaiman
In this captivating retelling, Neil Gaiman breathes new life into the ancient myths of Norse gods and heroes. His modern prose brings out the wit, tragedy, and timeless appeal of these stories, making them accessible to a wide audience.

The Gospel of Loki
By Joanne M. Harris
A unique retelling of Norse mythology from the perspective of **Loki**, the trickster god. Harris offers a fresh take on the myths, highlighting Loki's cunning and mischievous nature in a humorous and engaging narrative.

Further Reading on Viking Culture and Mythology:

The Children of Odin: The Book of Northern Myths
By Padraic Colum
A classic collection of Norse myths aimed at younger readers but equally engaging for adults. Colum's work is an excellent introduction to the major gods and their stories, written in a simple, accessible style.

The Norse Myths
By Kevin Crossley-Holland
This book offers a comprehensive retelling of the major Norse myths. Crossley-Holland's narrative is both vivid and faithful to the original sources, making it a valuable addition to any reader's collection.

The Saga of the Volsungs: The Norse Epic of Sigurd the Dragon Slayer
Translated by Jesse L. Byock
This saga recounts the epic tale of Sigurd and the dragon **Fafnir**, a story rich in heroism, betrayal, and magic. It is one of the most influential works in Norse literature and a must-read for anyone interested in heroic sagas.

RESOURCES FOR FURTHER STUDY

For those interested in diving deeper into Norse mythology, Viking culture, and the broader historical context of the myths, the following resources offer a wide range of perspectives. These tools will help you explore the origins of the myths, their historical significance, and their enduring impact on modern storytelling and culture.

Online Resources:

The Norse Mythology Blog
By Dr. Karl E. H. Seigfried
A comprehensive blog run by an expert in Norse mythology, offering articles, interviews, and discussions about the myths, their modern adaptations, and their influence on contemporary culture.
URL: www.norsemyth.org

The Viking Society for Northern Research
An academic organization that provides access to a wide range of texts related to Old Norse language, literature, and history. Their publications, including free scholarly articles, offer valuable insights into Viking culture and mythology.
URL: www.vsnr.org

The Mythic Norse World
A website dedicated to exploring the myths, gods, and creatures of Norse mythology. It includes detailed explanations of the Nine Realms, key deities, and mythological themes, along with maps and visual aids for better understanding the Norse cosmos.
URL: www.mythicnorseworld.com

Sacred Texts: Norse Mythology
Sacred Texts offers a collection of Norse myths, sagas, and related folklore, freely accessible online. This site includes translations of the **Poetic Edda** and **Prose Edda**, as well as other important texts

in the study of Norse mythology.
URL: www.sacred-texts.com/neu/ice/index.htm

The Skaldic Project
This academic resource focuses on Old Norse skaldic poetry, providing annotated texts, translations, and scholarly analysis. It's a valuable tool for those interested in the poetic tradition of the Vikings, which often intersects with mythological themes.
URL: skaldic.abdn.ac.uk

Old Norse Online
Hosted by the University of Texas at Austin, this resource provides language learning tools for Old Norse. For anyone interested in reading Norse mythology in its original language, this site offers grammar guides, texts, and translations.
URL: www.utexas.edu/cola/centers/lrc/eieol/norol-o-X.html

Museums and Cultural Institutions:

The National Museum of Denmark
The National Museum of Denmark houses extensive Viking collections, including artifacts, rune stones, and exhibits on Norse mythology. The museum's website offers virtual exhibits and educational resources for those unable to visit in person.
URL: www.natmus.dk/en

The Viking Ship Museum in Oslo, Norway
The Viking Ship Museum is a key resource for understanding Viking culture and mythology. Its exhibits include well-preserved Viking ships and artifacts that give insight into burial practices, many of which are deeply tied to Norse beliefs in the afterlife.
URL: www.khm.uio.no/english/visit-us/viking-ship-museum

Documentaries and Multimedia:

BBC's "The Vikings"
This documentary series explores Viking history and culture, including the myths and beliefs that shaped their worldview. It is a visually engaging introduction to Viking mythology and its impact on Scandinavian society.
Available through streaming platforms or the BBC.

The Mythology Podcast
This podcast covers myths from various cultures, with several episodes dedicated to Norse mythology. It's a great way to learn about the stories of **Odin, Thor, Loki,** and others while on the go.
URL: www.mythologypodcast.com

CrashCourse: Norse Mythology
This YouTube channel offers concise, engaging videos on a variety of academic subjects, including a dedicated episode on Norse mythology. These videos provide a quick and informative overview of the major gods, myths, and themes in a fun, accessible format.
URL: www.youtube.com/CrashCourse

ANSWER KEY

Mythology Quiz 1 Answers:

1. C) Ginnungagap
2. B) Muspelheim and Niflheim
3. C) Ymir
4. B) The sky
5. C) Yggdrasil
6. B) Nidhogg
7. D) Jotunheim

Mythology Quiz 2 Answers:

1. A) Vanaheim
2. D) Hel
3. C) Niflheim and Muspelheim
4. B) It is a realm associated with order and peace.
5. C) It is the bridge that souls cross to enter Helheim.
6. C) Svartalfheim

Mythology Quiz 3 Answers:

1. B) His eye
2. C) Mjolnir
3. C) Fenrir
4. B) Folkvangr
5. A) Gjallarhorn
6. B) Loki
7. C) Bifrost

Mythology Quiz 4 Answers:

1. C) A dragon
2. B) Gram
3. B) By tasting Fafnir's blood
4. C) In a snake pit

) "How the little piglets would grunt if they knew how the old boar suffers."

6. A) The Great Heathen Army

Mythology Quiz 5 Answers:

1. C) Hel
2. B) Einherjar
3. C) The sounding of Gjallarhorn
4. C) They are resurrected and feast in Odin's hall
5. C) Fenrir
6. A) Lif and Lifthrasir

Mythology Quiz 6 Answers:

1. A) Fenrir
2. B) Jormungandr
3. C) Choosers of the slain in battle
4. B) Gleipnir, a magical chain made from impossible materials
5. C) Beings who control the fate of gods and mortals
6. A) Ymir

Mythology Quiz 7 Answers:

1. B) A mistletoe dart
2. B) Freyja
3. C) His magical sword
4. A) That all beings in the Nine Realms must weep for him
5. B) It allows its practitioners to manipulate fate and see into the future
6. C) Thokk

Mythology Quiz 8 Answers:

1. B) J.R.R. Tolkien
2. B) Loki
3. B) God of War
4. B) Courage and honor in death
5. B) Odin
6. B) Ragnarok